Thomas Edward Bridgett

**The Discipline Of Drink**

An Historical Inquiry Into The Principles And Practices Of The Catholic...

Thomas Edward Bridgett

**The Discipline Of Drink**
An Historical Inquiry Into The Principles And Practices Of The Catholic...

ISBN/EAN: 9783744797887

Printed in Europe, USA, Canada, Australia, Japan

Cover: Foto ©ninafisch / pixelio.de

More available books at **www.hansebooks.com**

THE
# DISCIPLINE OF DRINK:

An Historical Inquiry into the Principles and Practice
of the Catholic Church

REGARDING THE

## USE, ABUSE, AND DISUSE OF ALCOHOLIC LIQUORS,

*Especially in England, Ireland, and Scotland,
from the 6th to the 16th Century.*

BY THE
### REV. T. E. BRIDGETT,
OF THE CONGREGATION OF THE MOST HOLY REDEEMER.

*PERMISSU SUPERIORUM.*

With an Introductory Letter to the Author,

BY

HIS EMINENCE CARDINAL MANNING,
ARCHBISHOP OF WESTMINSTER.

LONDON:
BURNS AND OATES,
17 AND 18 PORTMAN STREET, AND 63 PATERNOSTER ROW.
1876.

# PREFACE.

THE very first words recorded as spoken by St Peter, after the descent of the Holy Ghost on Pentecost, were these: "Ye men of Judea ... these are not drunk, as you suppose, seeing it is but the third hour of the day. But this is that which was spoken of by the prophet Joel: It shall come to pass, in the last days, saith the Lord, I will pour out of my Spirit upon all flesh" (Acts ii. 14-17). About thirty years later St Paul exhorted the Ephesians: "Be not drunk with wine, wherein is luxury, but be ye filled with the Holy Spirit" (Eph. v. 18). The Holy Spirit which animates the Christian Church, is thus distinctly contrasted by these two great apostles with drunkenness, which is enumerated among the works of the flesh (Gal. v. 21). Yet even from the beginning there were many among those once filled with the Holy Ghost in their baptism, who had driven Him from them, and in the terrible language of St Paul, "made a god of their belly, and were the enemies of the Cross of Christ" (Phil. iii. 18, 19). How such men have increased in number in the course of ages, and how they abound at the present day, is but too well known.

On the other hand, the same Spirit "manifestly foretold that in the last times some should depart from the faith;" and among their errors should teach a false abstinence from what God had created to be received with thanksgiving (1 Tim. iv. 1–3). In past ages, in their fanatical hatred of impurity, they condemned marriage; and at the present day, in the recoil from drunkenness, there are some who proscribe as sinful that "sober drinking, which is health to soul and body" (Ecclus. xxxi. 37).

The following pages are published in the

hope that they may be serviceable to the lay advocates of temperance, who, from want of accurate instruction in Christian morals, sometimes condemn drink which is the work of God, while attacking drunkenness which is the work of man. They will find in the first part of this inquiry what has been in all ages the teaching of the Catholic Church—taught herself by the Holy Ghost — on the subject of alcoholic drinks.

The book, however, is mainly historical rather than doctrinal; and will be found to contain a multitude of facts, both regarding the Catholic Church and the history of these countries, which are but little known, and yet are full of interest and instruction. The prevalence of drunkenness in the British Isles draws much attention at the present day. There are other vices both more heinous and more mischievous. But drunkenness is a palpable and public vice. It can be discussed in public, and treated of either morally, physically, or economically. The present little work is an attempt to treat it historically, at least in its moral aspects, and with a distinctly practical purpose. The writer was led to investigate, for his own guidance in the pulpit and the Confessional, the methods by which the vice of drunkenness has been met, in different ages and countries, by the Catholic Church. Out of the materials thus gathered he has made a selection. It was necessary to confine the theoretical part of such a subject within narrow limits, in order not to weary the reader; and to restrict the field of historical investigation, in order to arrive at sure and practical conclusions. After saying, therefore, what he has deemed sufficient on the general doctrine and discipline of the Church, he has followed out the subject into greater detail in the British Isles. He has chosen these countries both as more interesting to those who are likely to be his readers, and also because they offer a very favourable field for testing the influences of the Church. The inhabitants, of England at least, have always had both a propensity to the excessive use of stimulants, and the means of gratifying it. The Catholic Church also had almost undisputed possession for a thousand years of the religious reverence of these nations. What use did she make of it in the cause of

Temperance? If she made efforts, with what success were they attended?

These are questions, the solution of which must be interesting from many points of view. It should interest all as a contribution to that intimate history of the people, which is now becoming more relished than biographies of princes and records of battles, or of party strife. It has its controversial aspect, as bearing on the claims of the Catholic Church to divine assistance. And whether the efforts of the Church be considered a success or a failure, they are fraught with practical lessons for all who are now endeavouring to arrest the flood of national intemperance.

The writer wishes to state distinctly, from the outset, that he does not come forward as the advocate of any new theory, much less as the opponent of any work of zeal uncensured by the Catholic Church. He has stated such conclusions as he deemed certain, and has ventured to offer a few suggestions to his Catholic brethren. But, reserving his own judgment, he has neither attacked nor defended views on which Catholics are not yet agreed, or plans which have not yet stood the test of experience. As he respects the liberty of his brethren in the priesthood, so he writes with filial respect and submission to the teaching of the episcopate and the decisions of the Holy See.

# CONTENTS.

## PART I.
### DOCTRINE AND DISCIPLINE OF THE CHURCH IN GENERAL.

#### CHAPTER I.
DOCTRINE AS TO THE USE AND DISUSE OF ALCOHOLIC LIQUORS . . . . . . PAGE 1

#### CHAPTER II.
DOCTRINE AS TO THEIR ABUSE . . . . 23

#### CHAPTER III.
DISCIPLINE OF THE CHURCH . . . . 52

## PART II.
### THE PRECEDING DOCTRINE AND DISCIPLINE STUDIED IN THEIR RESULTS IN THE BRITISH ISLES.

#### CHAPTER IV.
DRUNKENNESS AN ENGLISH VICE . . 75

## CHAPTER V.
DRINKS USED IN FORMER TIMES . . . . 83

## CHAPTER VI.
DRINKING CUSTOMS . . . . . 99

## CHAPTER VII.
ACTION OF THE CIVIL POWER BEFORE THE SIXTEENTH CENTURY . . . . . . 118

## CHAPTER VIII.
ACTION OF THE CHURCH THROUGH THE SACRAMENT OF PENANCE . . . . . . 130

## CHAPTER IX.
REMARKS ON THE PENITENTIAL SYSTEM . . 152

## CHAPTER X.
ACTION OF THE CHURCH IN HER SYNODS . . 167

## CHAPTER XI.
RESULTS OF THE WITHDRAWAL OF THE CHURCH'S INFLUENCE . . . . . . 184

## CHAPTER XII.
CONCLUSIONS AND SUGGESTIONS . . . 198

APPENDIX CONTAINING RULES OF VARIOUS ASSOCIATIONS 231

INDEX . . . . . . . 257

# Introductory Letter to the Author,

BY

## HIS EMINENCE CARDINAL MANNING,
### ARCHBISHOP OF WESTMINSTER.

---

Archbishop's House, Westminster,
*June* 2, 1876.

My Dear Father Bridgett,

I HAVE read with great interest the proofs of your book on "The Discipline of Drink," as it has passed through the press. It is the first attempt to collect the counsels and judgments of Catholic pastors and writers on the use of wine, and on the sin of drunkenness. The historical part of your book is full of interest, and the quotations from the Fathers and the Saints are of great value and beauty. You have done well to quote them so copiously.

Your book will, I believe, be of signal use in clearing away a multitude of prejudices, and perhaps some more reasonable censures, which have impeded the efforts we are making to check the spread of intoxication.

So long as, and wheresoever, no Catholic associations existed, in which those who desire to save themselves by the help and support of others might unite together, it was inevitable that our people should enter into other societies not in the unity of the Catholic Church. My experience assures me that no counsel or influence on our part would suffice to prevent it; and so long as Catholics were associated in such fellowship, it was also inevitable that they would be induced to separate the practice of temperance or total abstinence from the use of the holy Sacraments and the practice of their religion.

Abstinence could not be put before them with the Catholic motives of penance, self-humiliation, reparation, and expiation for themselves and for others; and I am sorry to know that at times they were beset by great temptations to a spirit of self-consciousness and self-manifestation fatal to the spirit of penance. More than this, they could not help hearing a great deal of wild talk, worthy of the Manichees, and they were therefore in danger of learning the same language, if not of adopting also the same wild ideas.

Your book will show how broadly the Catholic

Church has always taught the lawfulness of using all things that God has made, in all their manifold combinations, so long as we use them in conformity to the law of God. Drunkenness is not the sin of the drink, but of the drunkard. Nevertheless, in every utterance of the Church, and in every page of Holy Scripture, wine is surrounded with warnings. The extreme facility of its abuse, its subtil fascination, its overpowering spells, and its stealthy imposition of bondage upon the intellect and the will, from the lowest to the highest natures, are all set forth in the Word of God, "as by the hand of a man writing upon the wall."

You have done well to point out that a new and more formidable agent of intoxication even than wine has in the last three centuries confirmed its grasp, I am ashamed to say, chiefly upon the Teutonic and Anglo-Saxon races. Alcohol has given intensity to the intoxicating power of wine, and when used in its undiluted strength has added a new madness to the evils of drunkenness. You have, therefore, as it seems to me, very wisely pointed out that no exact precedents can be found in the past action of the Church as to the way of dealing with an evil new in its kind, and so far more formidable both in its spread and in its intensity. But the principles of the

Church are always the same, and, in bringing forth things new and old, forms may vary, but the mind and action are immutable.

To meet the invasion of so widely extending an evil, it appears to me that a widely-extended organisation, specifically created for the purpose of arresting drunkenness, and of giving the mutual support of numbers and of sympathy to those who are in danger, is not only a wise mode of counteraction, but, I am inclined to believe, also a necessary provision. It affords external encouragement and support to multitudes who cannot stand alone.

I am glad to see that you have printed in the Appendix some words of mine, in which I expressed my hearty willingness to work with all Catholics who are labouring to extinguish drunkenness, whether they abstain altogether from all intoxicating drinks or not.

We are all pledged to temperance by our baptism; and with all those who labour to make that pledge a reality in themselves and in others I will always heartily work.

But I believe there are multitudes for whom a sharper discipline, and a more complete removal of all occasions and temptations to excess, are vitally necessary. So long as a man who has been in the habit or danger of intoxication continues to drink, the temptation to drink will be full upon him; so long as he continues to drink, he will go to places where drink is sold; so long as he goes to places where drink is sold, he will be habitually in the company of associates who will easily overpower his best resolutions. For such men I believe total abstinence to be almost the only hope; and what is true of men, I believe to be tenfold more true of women. And do not let us forget that at this moment drunkenness is spreading among our children, and that boys and girls are to be seen drunk in our streets; and that there are drinking-places habitually frequented by boys and girls of fourteen and fifteen years of age.

But you will not imagine that these dangers are to be found only among our poorer and our working population. King Pharaoh was raised up for one purpose, and King Solomon for another; but I have no desire in this letter to apply the example of King Solomon to modern society, except so far as to say that Solomon, with all his wisdom, would have been wiser if he had used total abstinence.

But my intention was to write you a letter, and not a treatise, and I will therefore add only one more word. When I see around me every day the wreck of men, women, and children, from the highest to the lowest class; the utter desolation of homes once happy and innocent, the destruction of the domestic life of the millions of our great working class, upon whom the whole fabric of our commonwealth must rest, I feel that temperance and total abstinence ought to be familiar thoughts in the mind even of those who have never in all their life been tempted to excess. If they would all consciously unite by example, by word, and by influence, to save those who are perishing in the dangers from which they are happily safe, many a soul, and many a home now hopelessly wrecked, would, I believe, be saved. When St. Paul told the Christians in Rome that it "is good not to eat flesh, and not to drink wine, nor anything whereby thy brother is offended, or scandalised, or made weak" (Rom. xiv. 21), he certainly did not intend to limit the wide reach of this principle of Christian charity to meats offered to idols. He meant what St. James meant when he said, "So speak ye, and so do, as being to be judged by the law of liberty" (St. James ii. 12). But the law of liberty is the law of charity; and if any self-denial on our part, in things that are lawful and to us altogether safe, shall help, or encourage, or support, or give even a shadow of strength to those to whom such lawful things are not only dangerous but often deadly, then assuredly the love of souls will prompt us to place ourselves at their side, and, in sharing their acts of self-denial, to give them a hand and a heart of sympathy.

Now I say this not as a precept, but as a counsel. If it be good, as St. Paul says it is, freely to forego lawful things for the sake of others, it is certainly good for us, of our own free will, to offer any little mortification we can in reparation, and expiation, and intercession for others. It is on this ground, as it seems to me, that total abstinence may be affirmed to be a wise and charitable use of our Christian liberty. And if, by laying on ourselves so slight a privation, we can in any way help those who are perishing, and those who are tempted, I do not think we shall ever have cause to regret that we freely chose that slight self-denial.

I thank you for your excellent book, and trust that it may powerfully help the work of saving souls from the pestilence of drink.

Believe me always, my dear Father Bridgett, yours affectionately in Jesus Christ,

HENRY EDWARD,
*Cardinal Archbishop of Westminster.*

# THE DISCIPLINE OF DRINK.

## Part the First.

*THE DOCTRINE AND DISCIPLINE OF THE CHURCH IN GENERAL.*

### CHAPTER I.

THE DOCTRINE AND DISCIPLINE OF THE CHURCH AS TO THE VOLUNTARY USE AND DISUSE OF ALCOHOLIC LIQUORS.

ALTHOUGH there can be no question whatsoever, as to the nature of the teaching of the Catholic Church, in all ages and countries, on the use and abuse of strong drinks, yet I shall multiply the evidence in this and the following chapters, because it is important at the present day, that the action of the Church in the cause of temperance should be clearly marked off from that of certain sects and associations, which seem to pursue the same end.

The earliest Christian writer who treats expressly of this subject, is Clement of Alexandria, the teacher of a school of Christian Philosophy in that famous seat of learning. In his Pedagogue, written about A.D. 195, he says:[1] "I praise and admire those who have chosen an austere life, who take water as the preserver of moderation, and flee wine like a threatening fire." He wishes that boys and girls, and young men and women, should use water. "But just as wine is fitter for evening when the air is cold, than for the midday heats, so also it may be used moderately to dispel the chill of old age." But wine has two purposes, the health of the body and the relaxation and exhilaration of the mind. He then shows the good effects, on the mind, of a moderate use of wine, adding that it should be mixed with plenty of water. "They are both the works of God, and the mixture of them tends to health. Life is made up by a mingling of what is necessary with what is useful; but what is necessary predominates over what is merely useful; so should water over wine."

After laying down rules of good breeding in the manner of drinking, he says—"The Scy-

[1] Book ii. ch. 2.

thians, Celts, Thracians, and all warlike nations, are most given to excessive drinking, and think this a beautiful and happy mode of life. But we, who are peaceable, drink from necessity or for friendship, not to excite anger and insolence. How do you think our Lord drank when He was made man for us? Was it impudently? Was it not temperately and decorously?"

He then proves by several passages of the Gospels, that our Lord did use wine, and concludes,—" This is a well settled and most certain thing with us against the Encratites."

One of the most famous disciples of Clement was Origen. In his commentary on the words of St Paul: "It is good not to eat flesh and not to drink wine, nor anything whereby thy brother is offended, or scandalised, or made weak" (Rom. xiv. 21), he writes: "These words —'It is good not to eat flesh nor to drink wine,' would have seemed to contradict what had gone before—that 'the kingdom of God is not meat and drink' (ver. 17)—had not the Apostle added immediately, 'nor anything whereby thy brother is offended.' For to eat flesh or not to eat it, to drink wine or not to drink it, are in themselves neither bad nor good, but indifferent. A bad man or an infidel can abstain from flesh and from wine, and it is certain that some do this in honour of their idols.

Sometimes also such abstinence is said to be prescribed to those who practise magic. Most certainly this is observed by many heretics. We do not say of such that it is good in them not to eat meat or drink wine.

"But on the other hand, to abstain from flesh and wine, in order that our brother be not offended, is by no means an indifferent thing, but a good thing. It is a good thing not to give scandal, as it is said: 'Be without offence to the Jews, and to the Gentiles, and to the Church of God' (1 Cor. x. 32). Let those then consider whether they act rightly, who try to force every one whom they find abstaining for any reason whatever, to eat flesh and drink wine, in order to remove from them the suspicion of superstitious adherence to distinctions of food. Let them reflect that the Apostle does not say: 'It is good to eat flesh and to drink wine,' but, on the contrary, 'it is good *not* to eat flesh and to drink wine, if in doing the contrary, your brother is offended.' The Apostle therefore is not willing that, for the sake of those who think they may eat, he should be forced to eat who is thereby offended; but rather, for the sake of him who thinks he should not eat, the Apostle bids those abstain who have no such fear."

That Origen is not here contemplating the

case of heretics, who abstain from meat or wine as if bad in themselves, is evident from what follows: "For there is danger lest, if the wall of abstinence be once broken down, he fall into the abyss of intemperance and excess, and afterwards make shipwreck of chastity. The one rule therefore is, that all be done 'that the work of God be not destroyed' (Rom. xiv. 20). Eat therefore, if your brother is edified thereby; do not eat, if by abstaining the work of God is advanced. Drink, if thereby your brother makes progress towards the faith; do not drink, if thereby either your brother suffers loss of faith, or you loss of charity."[1]

The same ancient writer gives a warning very necessary for our own days, when Temperance Societies are sometimes founded on doctrines like those of the ancient Gnostics, or on a basis of religious indifference. After quoting[2] the words: "In the last times some shall depart from the faith, giving heed to spirits of error, and doctrines of devils, speaking lies in hypocrisy . . . forbidding to marry, and (commanding) to abstain from meats which God hath created to be received with thanksgiving by the faithful" (1 Tim. iv. 1–3), Origen compares the teaching of these heretics to the lights which wreckers

---

[1] Origen in Ep. ad Rom., l. x. cap. 3.
[2] Ibid. cap. 5.

place on rocky and dangerous coasts. The unfortunate mariner, seeing the light, thinks that it betokens a safe harbour, and anxious to avoid the storm, he steers towards the light, and is wrecked among the breakers. So the Christian, tossed by the storm of intemperance, is deluded by the promises made to him by certain heretics, and while he seeks a safe harbour, makes shipwreck of his faith and of his soul. "Therefore," he concludes, "those who navigate the seas of this life, must not believe every light, but prove the spirits whether they be of God. For such false apostles are deceitful workmen, transforming themselves into the apostles of Christ" (2 Cor. xi. 13).

It will be seen from these passages of Clement and Origen, that already heresy had been taught, on the subject of the use of fermented liquors. The heresy had indeed a far wider range than the morality of drinking. But it seized on the notorious evils arising from the abuse of fermented liquors as a plausible basis for its false conclusions as to the evil nature of certain creatures and of their creator the Demiurgos. Modern errors have perhaps not much similarity with ancient Gnosticism. Yet to deny the lawfulness of the use of such liquors—to assert that alcohol is a kind of evil principle, and its use prohibited, *is* a heresy. It is to contradict the whole of the teaching of the Old and New Testaments, and the universal traditions of the Catholic Church. The teaching of her divine Founder began with the miracle of the conversion of water into wine at a marriage feast, and it concluded with the conversion of wine into His Blood, by which He instituted the perpetual marriage feast between Himself and His Church. The efforts of some modern sectarians to explain all this away, and to assert that the wine so often praised or promised in the Old Testament, and used by our Lord in the New Dispensation, was nothing but unfermented syrup, have been truly characterised as nothing less than "indecent."[1] There have been heresies on this subject from the beginning. Some of the early sects of Gnostics and Manichees forbade the use of wine even in the administration of the Holy Eucharist, substituting water or milk in its place. Tatian, who died in 174, was the founder of the Syrian heretics called Encratites, Hydroparastates or Aquarians alluded to by Clement. Similar sects appeared from time to time all through the Middle Ages. Catholic writers, therefore, while exhorting the faithful to voluntary abstinence, or to the observance of the restrictions of

[1] See article in *Westminster Review*, January 1875, "The Bible and Strong Drinks."

the Church on days of fasting, most carefully admonish them that in this they must not be moved by the false doctrines of heretics, or act as if they were still under the legal prohibitions of Judaism. They never cease to warn them that the true motives of abstinence are the subjugation of the flesh, obedience to lawful authority, or charity and condescension to others. "We warn those," says St Augustin, "who abstain from flesh-meat, not to look on the vessels in which flesh has been cooked as if (in Lent) they were unclean. 'All things are pure to the pure' (Tit. i. 15). The orthodox observance of Lent is for curbing the passions, not for shunning contamination. Hence those who, while they abstain from flesh, procure food of greater price, and requiring more careful cooking, greatly err." "You will see some, instead of their accustomed wine, procuring themselves unusual drinks, and while they refuse themselves the juice of the grape, compensating by a much sweeter decoction of other fruits." "This is not self-denial but a change of luxury. To the clean all things are clean, but luxury is clean in none."[1]

At the beginning of the twelfth century the old heresy of the Manichees reappeared among the sects of the Albigensians and Apostolics.

[1] St Aug. Serm. 205, 207, 209.

They found a vigorous opponent in St Bernard. "These men," he says in one of his sermons,[1] "are mere rustics and utterly contemptible; yet they must not be neglected, for their word spreads like a canker. They abstain from food that God made to be received with thanksgiving; and are heretics, not because they abstain, but because they abstain heretically. I too sometimes abstain; but to satisfy for my sins, not for superstition and impiety. St Paul chastised his body and brought it into subjection. I will abstain from wine, because in wine is luxury; or if I am weak I will use a little, according to the counsel of St Paul. I will abstain also from flesh-meat, lest by nourishing my own flesh too much I also nourish its vices. I will endeavour to take even bread in moderation, lest by overloading myself I be unfit for prayer. Nay I will not flood myself even with water. But it is not thus that heretics act. They make distinctions of food. If they are guided by physicians I do not blame their care of the flesh, if it is not excessive, 'for no one hateth his own flesh.' *If they are guided by spiritual physicians and ascetic discipline, I approve their virtue in taming the flesh and bridling its lusts.* But if they blame the good gifts of God, from the madness of the Manichees, and dare to call unclean what God

[1] Sermo 66 in Cantica.

created to be received with thanksgiving, then I execrate their blasphemy, and consider those unclean themselves who call God's works unclean. Woe to those who fear to defile their bodies with unclean food; the body of Christ, which is the Church, considers them unclean, and casts them forth. These heretics think that they alone are the body of Christ. Let those believe them, who are willing also to believe that they have the power, as they assert, to consecrate the body and blood of Christ at their own tables. And yet they would fain withdraw Christ from every class of men. They laugh at us for baptizing infants, for praying for the dead, for asking intercession of the saints. Thus they would refuse Christ to infants as if they were unfit by nature; *they refuse Him to adults by requiring from them an abstinence of which they are for the most part incapable.*[1] They would despoil the dead of the suffrages of the living, and they would despoil the living of the prayers of the saints."

But while attacking false principles of absti-

[1] It must not be forgotten, lest these words should be misunderstood, that those whom St Bernard was opposing demanded abstinence from meat as well as from fermented drinks, and that they exacted it from all as necessary to salvation. There is therefore no resemblance to the voluntary sacrifice asked in the Catholic Church from generous souls, or imposed for special reasons upon weak ones.

nence on the one side, the Church has to defend her own ascetic discipline from attacks from another quarter. A writer in one of our leading reviews, while opposing the teaching of the Good Templars, writes as follows :[1]—" That Jesus was a wine-drinker all through His course is plain. That His associates were wine-drinkers is equally plain. He Himself, in two notable passages, contrasts His conduct in this respect with that of John. The people, he tells us, jeered at Him as a wine-bibber. He makes no attempt to repudiate the accusation. It is evident that He had no sympathy whatever with the monkish asceticism which would seek to shelter itself under the shadow of His great name."

I am not sure that I understand the meaning of this last sentence. If by monkish asceticism the writer intends to describe the principles of Protestant Good Templars, against whom his article is directed, he confounds two things utterly antagonistic. It would be as reasonable to confound St John Baptist living in the desert with the demoniac who dwelt among the tombs.

But if, in bringing the teaching and example of our Lord to refute the opinions of the modern temperance fanatics, the writer thinks that he has, as it were by a side blow, despatched the

[1] *Westminster Review*, January 1875.

asceticism of the Catholic Church, on which the monastic life is based, he greatly mistakes the tendency of our Lord's words.

It is true that the Son of God draws out the contrast between the kind of life He had chosen for Himself, and that which His Spirit had taught the Baptist to adopt. But in doing so He is not proposing His own life as a more perfect one in its kind. In Him it was no doubt infinitely more perfect, so that St John was not worthy to loose the latchet of His shoe. It was the kind of life chosen by the Infinite Wisdom as most suited to the purposes of the Incarnation, and especially for manifesting the Divine Condescension. But our Lord Himself draws attention to the contrast, not for the purpose of comparison, but to point out the variety of the methods by which God sought to win His creatures, and the perversity of those who would be won by no method.

Let the reader examine the whole context of the eleventh chapter of St Matthew's Gospel.

In the first part there is the magnificent panegyric which our Lord makes of His precursor—" What went ye out into the desert to see? A man clothed in soft garments? Behold they that are in soft garments are in the houses of kings," &c. Surely this panegyric cannot be quoted as betraying "no sympathy whatever with monkish asceticism."

Next comes the reproach of the generation, which would neither dance when piped to, nor mourn in sympathy with lamentation, *i.e.*, which would neither yield to the condescension of the new Moses (see Acts iii. 22, 23) nor was awed by the austerities of the new Elias.

Later on, in the same chapter, our divine Master explains His purpose in eating and drinking in company with publicans and sinners. "Then began He to upbraid the cities wherein were done the most of His miracles, for that they had not done penance," saying that after witnessing miracles like His, Tyre and Sidon would have done penance in sackcloth and ashes. Sackcloth and ashes, as we know from the example of Nineveh, also praised by our Lord, were the accompaniments of a public fast. Hence we learn that, if our Lord sat at men's tables, and eat and drank as they did, it was that He might thus win their hearts, not to eating and drinking, but to sincere conversion, which would manifest itself in due time in self-denial and austerity. And if the conversion of His apostles was not followed immediately by multiplied fasts, the reason was, not that fasts were opposed to the spirit of His teaching, but that there is a time for everything, and that the absence of the

Bridegroom would be the occasion for austerities as His Presence had been a summons to spiritual joy (Luke v. 33–35).

Both forms of life, then, the more rigid one of St John and the more condescending one of Jesus Christ, had the same end—to invite men to penance. And as we are asked to study the spirit of our Lord, as if in opposition to that of St John, it may be as well to observe that there is a singular moderation in the demands of the austere Baptist. He does not bid the soldiers turn hermits, but to be content with their pay; nor the people to wear camel's hair garments, but to give to the poor their superfluous coats. He says nothing to them of his own diet of locusts and wild honey and water. He does not invite them to do penance in sackcloth and ashes. It would be then as reasonable to contrast the moderate demands of the Baptist with the severe requirements of Jesus Christ, as to contrast the unascetic life of our Lord with the "monkish asceticism" of St John. But, as the Divine Master said on this very occasion, "wisdom is justified by her children." The children of the Catholic Church have known how to admire one form of life without rejecting a contrary form. He who chooses celibacy disdains not the married state; and the married man can admit the superiority of celibacy without considering it a reproach to himself. The austerest saints have often been the most discreet and gentle directors. Each has his vocation from God. The most perfect life is not proposed to all. It is a more perfect thing to choose a less perfect life in accordance with one's duties or one's grace, than to emulate the better things which are beyond our reach.

Our first English cardinal, Robert Pullen, who was the friend of St Bernard, and one of the founders of the University of Oxford, writes very judiciously on these questions. "The Lord Jesus," he says,[1] "since He chose to live in the midst of men, did not refuse such food as men partake. He thus followed the rule which He gave to His apostles, to eat and drink whatever should be set before them. Those who live together in private may follow the more austere abstinence of St John, the dweller in the desert. But those who pass from place to place, and converse with the multitude, may imitate the example of apostolic condescension and moderation, knowing that 'the kingdom of God is not meat and drink' (Rom. xiv. 17). There is even greater merit to bridle one's appetite in abundance than to abstain in penury. Yet he who

[1] Libri Sententiarum, lib. viii. cap. 8.

is strongly tempted to excess will act more prudently if he shuns the occasion."[1]

The broad and varied wisdom which has always characterised the true Catholic traditions, may be illustrated from the life of the apostle St Paul. When preaching at Lystra, he told the heathens that in the past times God had not left Himself without testimony, "doing good from heaven, giving rains and fruitful seasons, filling our hearts with food and gladness" (Acts xiv. 16).

There are men whose minds are so narrow that, if they acknowledge the excellence of fasting, they will be quite unable to understand how the gladness arising from plenty can be anything but unholy. Yet, according to St Paul, it is a natural testimony to a bounteous Creator.

On the other hand, there are men who would catch at an expression like that of St Paul, to prove that the apostle had no sympathy whatever with monkish asceticism, and that if food and gladness bear testimony to a beneficent God,

[1] Lest those who imagine antagonism between St John and Jesus Christ, should suppose that the last English cardinal teaches differently from the first, I trust his Eminence, the present Archbishop of Westminster will forgive me for remarking that he might take the words of Cardinal Pullen as the motto of his temperance efforts: "Si cui tamen gula infesta est, copiam fugere securius est."

fasting and tears must be a worship only fit for a malignant Deity.

And yet St Paul and St Barnabas had been set apart, by command of the Holy Ghost, "in fasting and prayer," for this very missionary excursion, in which they speak to the heathen of "food and gladness" (Acts xiii. 2, 3), and, when they return to Lystra again, they tell their converts "that through many tribulations we must enter into the kingdom of God, and ordained them priests in prayer and fasting" (Acts xiv. 21, 22).

The Bridegroom was taken away, and the Holy Ghost was come. "Food and gladness" were not forbidden, but fasting and tears with spiritual joy were "a more excellent way."

I now shall give a few selections from writers of different ages and countries, to show how invariable has been the Church's teaching.

Julianus Pomerius was by nation a Moor, who went into Gaul about A.D. 500, and opened a school of rhetoric, and was ordained priest. He was a teacher of St Cæsarius of Arles. His treatise on the "Contemplative Life" was much read in the Middle Ages, when it was attributed to St Prosper. He thus writes:[1]—"Now, with regard to abstinence from wine or the use of it, what shall I say? The holy apostle has fixed

[1] De Vita Contemplativa, lib. ii. cap. 12.

the rule when he says: 'Be not drunk with wine wherein is luxury,' as though he had said, It is not the nature of wine but the excessive use of it which causes and nourishes impurity; therefore I do not prohibit you to use wine, but to be intoxicated with it, since the moderate use of wine strengthens a weak stomach, while drunkenness weakens both soul and body. To his disciple Timothy, who had injured himself by long abstinence, and disarranged his stomach by the use of water, he orders the use of a little wine: saying, 'Do not still drink water, but use a little wine for thy stomach's sake, and for thy frequent infirmities' (1 Tim. v. 23). According then to this, they in no way offend against abstinence who take wine, not for drunkenness, but only for the health of the body. Where there is no weakness it is good to abstain from wine, lest the indulgence which strengthens a weak body inflame a healthy one; though no one will say the use of wine is a sin any more than that of oil."

Further on, he says: " But since both Manichees and other heretics are able to abstain and to fast, detesting flesh as unclean, not for abstinence' sake, and using only bread and water, let us not consider it a great thing if we abstain from what they also reject; but where

[1] Cap. 24.

faith commends our abstinence and charity completes it. These virtues they have not, and therefore though they may kill themselves with their abstinence, edification and perfection they can never obtain.

"Again let us not, on account of our abstinence, prefer ourselves to those Catholic Christians who, either not being able or not being willing to abstain, receive with thanksgiving whatever God has granted to our use. Lest, if we boast, they be found to have more humility and other virtues, whereby they will be justly preferred to us who abstain. Let us then abstain from pride and boasting, the enemies of all virtues, that our abstinence and our fasts may be useful to us."

In the same spirit as the above passage are the words of St Gildas, a Briton and a monk, who wrote about the year 565. "Abstinence from food," he says,[1] "without charity is useless. Those who fast moderately, but carefully keep their heart pure before God, are better than those who eat no flesh, nor use horses or carriages (he is writing to monks), and on that account think themselves better than others. . . . They measure their bread, but boast without measure, drink only water, but quaff large draughts of hatred. . . . Our Lord pronounces those blessed who hunger and thirst after

[1] Epist. 2d. See Haddan and Stubbs. Councils i. p. 108.

justice, not those who drink water and despise their neighbours." St Isidore of Pelusium, an Egyptian of the fifth century, and a disciple of St Chrysostom, writes: "That to a weak stomach a little wine should be granted, is taught by St Paul; but to give wine, the hottest of liquids, to a strong man in the heat of youth, and him too a monk, certainly does not seem good, for it is to add fire to fire."[1]

But the same author writes to a monk:[2] "There is an abstinence which springs from hatred and evil dispositions. There is also an abstinence which belongs to the study and exercise of great and sublime virtues. If it is this latter which you follow, your fasting is blameless; but if you belong to the execrable sect of the Manichees and of Marcion, none of us will take food with you, since you corrupt the law of Christ, and scorn what is good as if it were evil."

St Antiochus, a monk in Palestine, at the beginning of the seventh century, writes:[3] "Take care in your abstinence not to hold any kind of food in abomination, for this would be execrable and like the malignity of the devils. For we do not abstain from any kind of food as if it were in its nature bad, but that by mode-

[1] Epist. lib. i. 385 (Migne, Patrol. Græca, tom. 78).
[2] Ibid. i. 52.    [3] Bib. Max. Lugd. t. xii. p. 222.

ration we may chastise our flesh, which is so easily inflamed; so that if our bodies are in good health they may be compelled to what is right and decent, and if they are sickly they may be strengthened by reasonable indulgence."

Nicetas of Constantinople, Bishop in Paphlagonia, in the ninth century, in his list of heresies, thus writes against Severianus [1]—" Severianus has picked up the ravings of former heresiarchs and added others of his own, teaching that men have to abstain altogether from the use of wine. He does not blush to say that the vine sprang from the embrace of the devil and the earth, and thus makes it the work of an evil spirit, whereas everything is made by God, and everything God made is good. Drunkenness, indeed, and the abuse of God's creatures, is bad. The sun also blinds those who fix their eyes on its orb, yet who on that account would despise the sun? Water refreshes and drowns. Fire warms and burns, and so with everything else. People have been choked by a morsel of bread, yet bread is a necessary of life, and strengthens the heart of man, and so also does wine if it is drunk properly and moderately, not going beyond the cup of temperance, or at least the second one of sufficiency; by which health is conferred on the body without injury to the

[1] Bib. Max. Lugd. t. xxv. p. 122.

soul. Did not Christ compare Himself to the vine and His disciples to the branches, and call His Father the vine dresser? And on the night of His betrayal, He took bread and a chalice filled with wine, and blessing both, He gave to us the New Testament, changing bread into His Body and wine into His Blood. United to us by these two, He remains with us all days even as He promised.

"This Severianus who abominates both wine and marriage, shows himself by the one blasphemy unworthy to have been born, and by the other unworthy of the chalice of the Lord. But Christ blessed both by His presence at the marriage-feast of Cana, and by changing water into wine."

I have not scrupled to give these long quotations, that it may be seen what were the true principles of asceticism taught in the Catholic Church by monks in the dark ages, as well as by the philosophical writers of the school of Alexandria; and on which were founded celibacy, fasting, abstinence from strong drinks, or whatever other austerity the Church has sanctioned. The Church never blamed God as the author of sin, or counted any of His creatures evil; and would not tolerate that those who abstained should pass censure on those who used their liberty.

## CHAPTER II.

#### DOCTRINE OF THE CHURCH ON DRUNKENNESS.

IT is sometimes supposed that drunkenness, as a wide-spread, popular vice, is a new evil, and one with which the Church has never before had to contend. And it is probably true that in our great cities, and from the present development of commerce and manufacture, it has assumed proportions beyond anything known in former ages. Still no one can have read the homilies of St Chrysostom, of St Augustin, or of St Cæsarius, without seeing that, even in the fourth and fifth centuries of the Christian Church, there were multitudes in Asia, Africa, and Europe, whom drunkenness made the enemies of the cross of Christ which they professed to revere. Let us begin with Africa in the fourth century.

"How many thieves," exclaims St Augustin, "how many drunkards, how many calumniators, how many theatre-goers! Do not the same persons now fill the churches who fill the theatres? And often, by their clamour, they show that they seek in the churches the very same objects that they seek in the theatres."[1]

In another sermon, after having asked triumphantly, "Where are now the enemies of the martyrs?" he is obliged to check himself and add with sorrow, "Yet the drunkards now persecute with their cups those whom the pagans formerly persecuted with stones."[2]

"You know," he says elsewhere, "that there are sober men; *they are few indeed*, yet there are such. You know also that there are drunkards, plenty of them;"[3] and he tells us that in his time the people had grown accustomed to speak of drunkenness, not only without horror but even laughingly."[4]

Drunkenness had even found its slaves in the ranks of the clergy. In discussing the question of baptism administered by a sinner, St Augustin proposes the case of a priest or deacon addicted to drunkenness, and says that he selects such an one purposely; "because drunkenness is a vice men cannot conceal, and that not even a blind man can be ignorant how many are addicted to

---

[1] Sermo 252, tom. v. p. 1640.
[2] Enar. in Ps. lix. tom. iv. p. 585.
[3] Sermo 151, tom. v. p 719.
[4] De Bap. c. Donat. tom. ix. p. 137.

it." He asks pardon ironically of his Donatist adversary for supposing that there could be drunken priests in his sect which affected such purity; and yet, he says, "this pestilence of souls has spread its ravages so far and wide, that I should be indeed surprised if it had not found its way even into your little flock, though you do boast as if you had separated the goats from the sheep, even before the coming of the Good Shepherd."[1]

The vice of intemperance had indeed become so common in Africa as greatly to disturb the discipline of the Church. "Who is there now," says the saintly Doctor,[2] "who does not think lightly of the sin of habitual drunkenness? That sin abounds, and is thought little of. The heart of the drunkard has lost all feeling. It has lost all sense of pain, and consequently all hope of recovery. If a thing feels pain when it is pricked, it is either healthy or at least gives hope that it may become healthy. But when a member has no feeling, though it is pinched or pricked, it may be considered dead and cut off from the body. Yet we sometimes are lenient, and can only employ words; we are loth to excommunicate and cast out of the Church; for we fear lest he who is chastised should be made worse by the chastisement. And though such are already dead

[1] Ep. 93.     [2] Serm. 17, tom. v. p. 95.

in soul, yet since our Physician is almighty we must not despair of them, but pray with all our strength that the Lord may open the ears of their hearts which they keep closed."

There were some abuses, however, with which the saint could not temporise. The very churches were profaned by drunkenness; and against this scandal St Augustin strove, and not in vain. There are two letters in which he has given us a detailed history of the origin and growth of the abuse, of his own plans, hopes, and fears, and of his final triumph. Though they are long, yet those who have at heart the extirpation of our present scandals, and are perhaps little sanguine of success, will read with deep interest the account of this ancient battle, and will feel animated by it to do valiantly themselves.

The first letter is addressed to Aurelius, who had just become Bishop of Carthage. It was written in the year 392, when St Augustin was still only a priest, though the care of the Church of Hippo in many respects had been imposed on him.

After the introduction he thus enters on the subject of his letter:—" St Paul enumerates three sorts of crimes. He writes: 'Not in rioting and drunkenness, not in chambering and impurities, not in contention and envy' (Rom.

xiii. 13). Now what he puts here in the second place (impurity), is most severely punished in the Church, while the first and last seem to men to be tolerated, so that by degrees it might come to pass that they would be no longer esteemed as vices. Yes! Impurity is considered so enormous a crime, that no one who has defiled himself with such a sin is esteemed worthy, I do not say of the sacred ministry, but even of the reception of the sacraments. This is quite right. Yet why those only who are guilty of this crime? Feasting and drunkenness seem so permitted, that not only on great days, but day after day, they are kept up in honour of the most blessed martyrs. Were not this a sacrilege as well as a turpitude, it might perhaps seem tolerable. And yet what would then become of the authority of the Apostle, who mentions drunkards among the great criminals with whom we should not so much as eat bread? (1 Cor. v. 11). But if we are to bear patiently such crimes committed in private, and even to receive the Body of Christ with men with whom we are forbidden so much as to eat bread, yet at least let the disgrace be kept from the tombs of the holy martyrs, from the place of the holy sacraments, and the houses of prayer. Who will dare to blame in private what, when it is done in holy places, is called honour to the martyrs?

"Were Africa the first to rise up against such a scandal, it would be worthy of imitation. But this is far from being the case. Throughout the greater part of Italy, and in nearly all foreign churches, the scandal does not exist, either because it never had a beginning, or because at its first outset, or even after it had become inveterate, it has been abolished by the zeal of holy bishops. This ought to give us courage. . . .

"Yet the pestilence is of such a magnitude, that it seems to me it cannot be cured except by the authority of a Council. Or at least, if one Church must begin, it should be that of Carthage. It would seem like audacity to try to change what Carthage retains; but it would be great impudence to retain what the Church of Carthage had corrected. And for this work what bishop could be more fit than he who, even when a deacon, execrated the scandal?

"What you then grieved over, must now be removed—not harshly, but, as it is written, 'in the spirit of meekness' (Gal. vi. 1). Your letters, so full of charity, give me boldness to discuss this matter with you, as if I were talking with myself. I think then that these abuses must be removed, not imperiously, nor harshly ; by instruction rather than by precept, by persuasions rather than by threats. It is thus one must act in a multitude: we may be severe towards the sins of a few. If we use any threats, let it be done with sorrow, alleging future penalties from Holy Scripture, that God may rather be feared in our words, then we ourselves in our authority. Thus first the spiritual will be moved, or those who are nearly spiritual, and afterwards by their authority, and gentle yet urgent admonitions, the multitude will be induced to give way.

But since this drinking and luxurious feasting in cemeteries are by the carnal and ignorant people not only considered to be honour offered to the martyrs, but also solace to the dead, it seems to me that we shall more easily dissuade them from their scandalous excesses, if while they are prohibited by authority of Scripture, the oblations for the souls of the faithful departed, which we must in truth believe to be efficacious, be not laid pompously on the shrines of the martyrs, but be given freely and without display to all who ask; and that there be no sale of the oblations; but if any one, out of a spirit of religion, wishes to make an offering in money, let it be given at once to the poor. By this means they will not appear to be neglecting the memory of their dead (which would cause them great grief), and no celebration will take place in the Church but what is pious and decent."

(He then goes on to speak of contention and pride.)[1]

We do not know what steps were taken at Carthage by Aurelius, in consequence of this letter. But an African canon, of which the precise date is unknown, was probably the result. It runs thus: " No bishops or clergy may feast in the church, unless they take refreshment there when passing through a city, having no other place of entertainment. The people also must be restrained from such feasts as much as possible." [2]

However, three years after his letter to Aurelius, St Augustin had the authority of his own bishop to attack the evil customs, and he has related in a letter to his friend Alypius, Bishop of Thagaste, all the circumstances.

He begins by attributing his success to his friend's prayers, and then continues as follows:[3]—

"Therefore let me not fail to relate to your charity what has taken place; so that, as you joined us in pouring out prayers for this mercy before it was obtained, you may now join us in

---

[1] Tom. ii. p. 28. Ep. 22.
[2] Labbe. Conc., tom. ii. col. 1069.
[3] I avail myself in this letter of the excellent translation of the Rev. Marcus Dods, vol. i. p. 84–92.

rendering thanks for it after it has been received. When I was informed after your departure that some were becoming openly violent, and declaring that they could not submit to the prohibition (intimated while you were here) of that feast which they call Lœtitia, vainly attempting to disguise their revels under a fair name, it happened most opportunely for me, by the hidden fore-ordination of the Almighty God, that on the fourth day of the week that chapter of the Gospel fell to be expounded in ordinary course, in which the words occur: 'Give not that which is holy to dogs; neither cast ye your pearls before swine' (Matt. vii. 6). I discoursed therefore concerning dogs and swine in such a way, as to compel those who clamour with obstinate barking against the divine precepts, and who are given up to the abominations of carnal pleasures, to blush for shame; and followed it up by saying that they might plainly see how criminal it was to do, under the name of religion, within the walls of the church, that which, if it were practised by them in their own houses, would make it necessary for them to be debarred from that which is holy, and from the privileges which are the pearls of the Church.

"Although these words were well received, nevertheless, as few had attended the meeting, all had not been done which so great an emergency required. When, however, this discourse was, according to the ability and zeal of each, made known abroad by those who had heard it, it found many opponents. But when the morning of Quadragesima came round, and a great multitude had assembled at the hour of exposition of Scripture, that passage in the Gospel was read in which our Lord said, concerning those sellers who were driven out of the temple, and the tables of the money-changers which He had overthrown, that the house of His Father had been made a den of thieves instead of a house of prayer. After awakening their attention by bringing forward the subject of immoderate indulgence in wine, I myself also read this chapter, and added to it an argument to prove with how much greater anger and vehemence our Lord would cast forth drunken revels, which are everywhere disgraceful, from that temple from which He thus drove out merchandise lawful elsewhere, especially when the things sold were those required for the sacrifices appointed in that dispensation; and I asked them whether they regarded a place occupied by men selling what was necessary, or one used by men drinking to excess, as bearing the greater resemblance to a den of thieves.

"Moreover, as passages of Scripture which I had prepared were held ready to be put into my hands, I went on to say that the Jewish nation, with all its lack of spirituality in religion, never held feasts, even temperate feasts, much less feasts disgraced by intemperance, in their temple, in which at that time the Body and Blood of the Lord were not yet offered, and that in history they are not found to have been excited by wine on any public occasion bearing the name of worship, except when they held a feast before the idol which they had made. While I said these things I took the manuscript from the attendant, and read that whole passage. Reminding them of the words of the Apostle, who says, in order to distinguish Christians from the obdurate Jews, that they are his epistle written, not in tables of stones, but in the fleshy tables of the heart; I asked further, with the deepest sorrow, how it was that, although Moses the servant of God broke both the tables of stone because of these rulers of Israel, I could not break the hearts of those who, though men of the New Testament dispensation, were desiring in their celebration of saints' days, to repeat often the public perpetration of excesses of which the people of the Old Testament economy were guilty only once, and that in an act of idolatry.

"Having then given back the manuscript of Exodus, I proceeded to enlarge, so far as my time permitted, on the crime of drunkenness, and took up the writings of the Apostle Paul, and showed among what sins it is classed by him, reading the text—'If any man that is named a brother, be a fornicator, or covetous, or a server of idols, or a railer, or a drunkard, or an extortioner; with such an one, not so much as to eat' (1 Cor. v. 11); pathetically reminding them how great is our danger in eating with those who are guilty of intemperance, even in their own houses. I read also what is added a little further on in the same epistle: 'Do not err: Neither fornicators, nor idolaters, nor adulterers, nor the effeminate, nor liers with mankind, nor thieves, nor covetous, nor drunkards, nor railers, nor extortioners shall possess the Kingdom of God. And such some of you were; but you are washed, but you are sanctified, but you are justified in the name of our Lord Jesus Christ, and the Spirit of our God.' After reading these, I charged them to consider how believers could hear these words, 'but you are washed,' if they still tolerated in their own hearts—that is, in God's inner temple—the abominations of such lusts as these against which the Kingdom of Heaven is shut. Then I went on to that passage, 'When you come therefore together into one place, it is not now to eat of the Lord's Supper. For every one taketh before his own supper to eat. And one indeed is hungry, and another is drunk. What, have you not houses to eat and to drink in? Or despise ye the Church of God?' After reading which, I more especially begged them to remark that not even innocent and temperate feasts were permitted in the Church; for the Apostle said not, 'Have you not houses of your own in which to be drunken?' as if it was drunkenness alone which was unlawful in the Church; but, 'Have you not houses to eat and drink in?'—things lawful in themselves, but not lawful in the Church, inasmuch as men have their own houses in which they may be recruited by necessary food; whereas now, by the corruption of the times and the relaxation of morals, we have been brought so low that, no longer insisting upon sobriety in the houses of men, all that we venture to demand is, that the realm of tolerated excess be restricted to their own homes.

"I reminded them also of a passage in the Gospel which I had expounded the day before, in which it is said by the false prophets—'By their fruits you shall know them.' I also bade them remember that in that place our works are signified by the word fruits. Then I asked among what kind of fruits drunkenness was named, and read that passage in the Epistle to the Galatians—'Now the works of the flesh are manifest, which are fornication, uncleanness, immodesty, luxury, idolatry, witchcrafts, enmities, contentions, emulations, wraths, quarrels, dissensions, sects, envies, murders, drunkenness, revellings, and such like. Of the which I foretel you, as I have foretold to you, that they who do such things shall not obtain the Kingdom of God.' After these words I asked how, when God has commanded that Christians be known by their fruits, we could be known as Christians by this fruit of drunkenness? I added—'But the fruit of the Spirit is love, joy, peace, longsuffering, gentleness, goodness, faith, meekness, temperance;' also, that we must read what follows there—'But the fruit of the Spirit is charity, joy, peace, patience, benignity, goodness, longanimity, mildness, faith, modesty, continency, chastity.' And I pleaded with them to consider how shameful and lamentable it would be, if, not content with living at home in the practice of these works of the flesh, they even wished by them, forsooth, to honour the Church, and to fill the whole area of so large a place of worship, if they were permitted, with crowds of revellers and drunkards; and yet would not present to God those fruits of the Spirit which, by the authority of Scripture, and by my groans, they were called to yield, and by the offering of which they would most suitably celebrate the Saints' days.

"This being finished, I returned the manuscript; and being asked to speak, I set before their eyes with all my might, as the danger itself constrained me, and as the Lord was pleased to give strength, the danger shared by them who were committed to my care, and by me, who must give account to the Chief Shepherd, and implored them by His humiliation, by the unparalleled insults, the buffetings and spitting on the face which He endured, by His pierced hands and crown of thorns, and by His cross and blood, to have pity on me at least, if they were displeased with themselves, and to consider the inexpressible love cherished towards me by the aged and venerable Valerius, who had not scrupled to assign to me for their sakes the perilous burden of expounding to them the word of truth, and had often told them that in my coming here his prayers were answered; not rejoicing, surely, that I had come to share or to behold the death of our hearers, but rejoicing that I had come to share his labours for their eternal life. In conclusion, I told them that I was resolved to trust in Him who cannot lie, and who has given us a promise by the mouth of the prophet, saying of our Lord Jesus Christ, 'And if his children forsake my law, and walk not in my judgments, if they profane my justices, and keep not my commandments, I will visit their iniquities with a rod, and their sins with stripes. But my mercy I will not take away from him.' I declared therefore that I put my trust in Him, that if they despised the weighty words which had now been read and spoken to them, He would visit them with the rod and with stripes, and not leave them to be condemned with the world. In this appeal I put forth all the power in thought and utterance which, in an emergency so great and hazardous, our Saviour and Ruler was pleased to supply. I did not move them to weep by first weeping myself; but while these things were being spoken, I own that, moved by the tears which they began to shed, I myself could not refrain from following their example. And when we had thus wept together, I concluded my sermon with full persuasion that they would be restrained by it from the abuses denounced.

"Next morning, however, when the day dawned, which so many were accustomed to devote to excess in eating and drinking, I received notice that some, even of those who were present when I preached, had not yet desisted from complaint, and that so great was the power of detestable custom with them, that, using no other argument, they asked, 'Wherefore is this now prohibited? Were they not Christians who in former times did not interfere with this practice?' On hearing this I knew not what more powerful means for influencing them I could devise; but resolved, in the event of their judging it proper to persevere, that after reading in Ezekiel's prophecy that the watchman has delivered his own soul if he has given warning, even though the persons warned refuse to give heed to him, I would shake my garments and depart. But then the Lord showed me that He leaves us not alone, and taught me how He encourages us to trust Him; for before the time at which I had to ascend the pulpit, the very persons, of whose complaint against interference with long-established custom I had heard, came to me. Receiving them kindly, I by a few words brought them round to a right opinion; and when it came to the time for my discourse, having laid aside the lecture which I had prepared as now unnecessary, I said a few things concerning the question mentioned above—' Wherefore *now* prohibit this custom?' Saying that to those who might propose it the briefest and best answer would be this—' Let us now at last put down what ought to have been earlier prohibited.'

"Lest, however, any slight should seem to be put by us on those who, before our time, either tolerated or did not dare to put down such manifest excesses of an undisciplined multitude, I explained to them the circumstances out of which this custom seems to have necessarily risen in the Church; namely, that when, in the peace which came after such numerous and violent persecutions, crowds of heathen who wished to assume the Christian religion were kept back, because, having been accustomed to celebrate the feasts connected with their worship of idols in revelling and drunkenness, they could not easily refrain from pleasures so hurtful and so habitual, it had seemed good to our ancestors, making for the time a concession to this infirmity, to permit them to celebrate, instead of the festivals which they renounced, other feasts in honour of the holy martyrs, which were observed, not as before with a profane design, but with similar self-indulgence. I added, that now upon them as persons bound together in the name of Christ, and submissive to the yoke of His august authority, the wholesome restraints of sobriety were laid—restraints with which the honour and fear due to Him who appointed them should move them to comply—and that, therefore, the time had now come in which all who did not dare to cast off the Christian profession should begin to walk according to Christ's will; and being now confirmed Christians, should reject those concessions to infirmity which were made only for a time in order to their becoming such.

"I then exhorted them to imitate the example of the churches beyond the sea, in some of which these practices had never been tolerated, while in others they had been already put down by the people complying with the counsel of good ecclesiastical rulers; and as the examples of daily excess in the use of wine in the Church of the blessed Apostle Peter were brought forward in defence of the practice, I said in the first place, that I had heard that these excesses had been often forbidden, but because the place was at a distance from the bishop's control, and because in such a city the multitude of carnally-minded persons was great, the foreigners especially, of whom there is a constant influx, clinging to that practice with an obstinacy proportioned to their ignorance, the suppression of so great an evil had not yet been possible. If, however, I continued, we would honour the Apostle Peter, we ought to hear his words, and look much more to the epistles by which his mind is made known to us, than to the place of worship, by which it is not made known; and immediately taking the manuscript, I read his own words: 'Christ, therefore, having suffered in the flesh, be you also armed with the same thought: for he that hath suffered in the flesh, hath ceased from sins; that now he may live the rest of his time in the flesh, not after the desires of men, but according to the will of God. For the time past is sufficient to have fulfilled the will of the Gentiles, for them who have walked in riotousness, lusts, excess of wine, revellings, banquetings, and unlawful worshipping of idols.' After this, when I saw that all were with one consent turning to a right mind, and renouncing the custom against which I had protested, I exhorted them to assemble at noon for the reading of God's word and singing of psalms; stating that we had resolved thus to celebrate the festival in a way much more accordant with purity and piety; and that, by the number of worshippers who should assemble for this purpose, it would plainly appear who were guided by reason, and who were the slaves of appetite. With these words the discourse concluded.

" In the afternoon a greater number assembled than in the forenoon, and there was reading and praise alternately up to the hour at which I went out in company with the bishop; and after our coming two psalms were read, then the old man [Valerius] constrained me by his express command to say something to the people; from which I would rather have been excused, as I was longing for the close of the anxieties of the day. I delivered a short discourse in order to express our gratitude to God. And as we heard the noise of the feasting, which was going on as usual in the church of the heretics, who still prolonged their revelry while we were so differently engaged, I remarked that the beauty of day is enhanced by contrast with the night, and that when anything black is near, the purity of white is the more pleasing; and that, in like manner, our meeting for a spiritual feast might perhaps have been somewhat less sweet to us, but for the contrast of the carnal excesses in which the others indulged; and I exhorted them to desire eagerly such feasts as we then enjoyed, if they had tasted the goodness of the Lord. At the same time, I said that those may well be afraid who seek anything, which shall one day be destroyed as the chief object of their desire, seeing that every one shares the portion of that which he worships; a warning expressly given by the Apostle to such, when he says of them their 'god is their belly;' inasmuch as he has elsewhere said, 'Meat for the belly, and the belly for meats; but God shall destroy both it and them.' I added, that it is our duty to seek that which is imperishable, which, far removed from carnal affections, is obtained through sanctification of the spirit; and when those things which the Lord was pleased to suggest to me had been spoken on this subject as the occasion required, the daily evening exercises of worship were performed; and when with the bishop I retired from the church, the brethren said a hymn there, a considerable multitude remaining in the church and engaging in praise even till daylight failed. I have thus related as concisely as I could that which I am sure you longed to hear. Pray that God may be pleased to protect our efforts from giving offence or provoking odium in any way."

The history which St Augustin has so graphically related is but an incident in the secular warfare of the Church. She is ever militant, and if an abuse is suppressed in one country it springs up in another, or in the same after a few generations.

I am not attempting to write a history of drunkenness. It would be neither pleasant nor profitable. But it may be useful to study the action of the Church for a few centuries in some of the countries of Europe, before confining our attention (as I propose to do afterwards) to the British Isles. I begin with Gaul.

The picture which St Cæsarius of Arles gives us of the state of Provence in the beginning of the sixth century is rather startling. We must notice, however, that though it had long been Christian, it had been recently overrun by barbarians, and was then under the dominion of the Visigoths. As then the saint is addressing a recently-converted and half-civilised people, we may, from what he says, form some conception of the condition of our own Saxon and Danish ancestors, and of the discourses which would have been addressed to them. I will give portions of one of these sermons.[1] "Although, beloved brethren, by the mercy of Christ, I well believe that you fear the gulf of drunkenness like the pit of hell itself"—it is thus he begins —"and that not only you are resolved to abstain from excess yourselves, but you will not press or force others to take more than is right; yet, as there must always be some who are negligent, I must beg you who are sober, and who allow no drunkenness at your tables, not to take offence at me, because I find it necessary to rebuke others who are given to this vice.

"For though drunkenness is indeed a great evil, and a heinous vice and hateful to God, yet it has been so spread by custom throughout the world, that by some, who care not to know the commands of God, it is not thought or believed to be a sin at all; so that they ridicule in their feasts those who cannot drink as much as others, and are not ashamed, by a cruel kind of friendship, to compel men to take more than they require. It were less cruel to wound a man's

[1] In Appendice ad Serm. St Aug. 294.

body with a sword than thus to slay his soul by drunkenness.

"Our bodies being made of earth may be compared with earth. Now, when there has been too much rain, the earth becomes soaked and muddy and cannot be tilled. Just so our body, when inebriated with excessive drink, can receive no spiritual culture and produce no fruits such as the soul needs. Drunkards indeed are like marshes, You know what marshes produce—leeches, frogs, worms which make us shudder, useless reeds and grasses, which have every year to be set on fire; but nothing useful, nothing fit to eat. So, too, whatever springs from drunkenness is only fit for the fire."

Then, after a vivid description of the effects of drunkenness, he continues, "Yet these men excuse themselves, saying, 'I shall offend my friend, if when I invite him I do not give him as much as he desires.' I reply that you should not have such friends, who are God's enemies, and make you such also. Is it wise thus to cling to a drunkard and to be separated from God? At least, then, do not press and force him to drink; if he wishes to get drunk let him do it himself and perish alone. Oh, what a wretched world is this! Men force drunkards to go on drinking, and will not give one cup to the poor man who begs at their door."

## *Drunkenness.*

He continues, by many arguments and passages of Scripture, to show the evil and its punishments.

In another sermon,[1] though he admits that there are many who know how to keep sober tables, yet he says that there are rich gluttons who even order salt meats to be prepared to excite their thirst the more. "Oh!" he exclaims, "if the pagans who know not God did such things, we should not wonder; but how can Christians be guilty of such shame whom God has called out of darkness into His admirable light, and from death to life? By the tremendous judgment of God, I adjure you be not like the pagans in drunkenness if you are unlike them in faith; for even though you should not commit other crimes, yet drunkenness, if it is frequent, and not amended and repented of, casts into the depths of hell, according to what is said: Drunkards shall not possess the kingdom of God . . . Alas! how will priests have to render account at the day of judgment for their people if they leave them in ignorance of the greatness of this sin, and do not frequently preach to them of its fearful consequences. . . .

"And again, how sad and shameful a thing is related of some of the country people, that when they have wine, or have made some other

[1] In Appendice ad Serm. St Aug. 295.

kind of drink, they invite their neighbours to a drinking party, and keep them four or five days together, not letting them go back home till all the drink is consumed; wasting thus in these shameful potations what ought to have sufficed during two or three months for themselves and their families.

"As for me, then, while I with all humility, with great love and paternal solicitude thus warn you, I clear my conscience before God. He who listens to me willingly, and obeys faithfully what I have said, shall have an eternal reward; but let him who despises my words, fear lest he incur eternal punishment. Yet I trust in the mercy of God, that all drunkards will so return to sobriety by the grace of God, as to cause joy to us now, and gain eternal reward for themselves hereafter."

The hopes thus expressed by St Cæsarius do not seem to have been altogether vain; for when a century and a half later St Boniface visited the continent, he did not find the vice of drunkenness prevalent in Provence or in Gaul, in Lombardy, or among the Franks.

It will be enough on such a subject to give one more specimen. It is from a sermon composed expressly as a model for priests who had the care of the recently-converted Saxons.

Rabanus Maurus thus preached in Germany in the beginning of the ninth century:

"There are some vices, dearest brethren, which, though very great, yet in our days to some appear so small, that they reckon them either the least of evils or no evils at all. They have so spread by the abuse of men that instead of being blamed as crimes and sins, they are praised as if they were virtues. Of such abandoned men, the prophet said (Isa. iii. 9). 'They have proclaimed abroad their sin as Sodom, and they have not hid it.' But the Lord returned them by this prophet an answer worthy of their error: 'Woe to you that call evil good, and good evil; that put darkness for light, and light for darkness; that put bitter for sweet, and sweet for bitter' (Isa. v. 20).

"Among these vices feasting and drunkenness especially reign, since not only the rude and vulgar people, but the noble and powerful of the land, are given up to them. Both sexes and all ages have made intemperance into a custom. 'For the sinner is praised in the desires of his soul, and the unjust man is blessed' (Ps. ix. 24 or x. 3). And so greatly has this plague spread that it has infected some of our own order in the priesthood, so that not only they do not correct the drunkards, but become drunkards themselves. Oh! what wickedness is this, brethren, what bitter evil is this, which does not leave unhurt even rulers and dignities, until virtues are spoken ill of, and vices extolled? For the saying is of those who are given to drunkenness: 'They are generous, and know what is due to mercy and to charity;' as if it were mercy and charity to deceive one's self and to drag others with us to perdition. Did the Apostle St Paul preach such charity as this? Is this the charity of which he said: 'Charity is patient, is kind; charity envieth not, dealeth not perversely, is not puffed up, rejoiceth not in iniquity, but rejoiceth with the truth' (1 Cor. xiii. 4, 5)?

"Tell me, you who praise feasting and drunkenness, whether it is a good thing or an evil, to extinguish the light of the mind by excess, to disturb the reason, to obscure the sight, to lose speech and the use of the limbs, and to become like a madman or one possessed? Did God make man thus? Is this the glory of God's image of which it is written: God made man to His own likeness? What an intolerable blasphemy would it be to assert such a thing, when God is supremely good and alone blessed and powerful, the King of kings and Lord of lords. 'He saw all things that He had made, and behold they were very good.' Hence drunkenness was not made by Him"[1] . . .

[1] Rabani opera. Homil. 63. Migne. tom. 110. col. 119.

Such was the language addressed by the great prelates to their flocks in the early ages. It has been repeated from age to age from myriads of pulpits to the present day, and will continue to be the topic of the preacher until the day when "the Son of man shall send His angels, and they shall gather out of His kingdom all scandals, and them that work iniquity" (Matt. xiii. 41).

# CHAPTER III.

#### THE CHURCH'S DISCIPLINE.

THE Church has been compared by her Divine Founder to a field in which weeds will grow amidst the wheat until the harvest. Yet if the weeds are tolerated it is for the sake of the wheat, or it is in the hopes that, by a miracle of God's power and mercy, the weeds may even become wheat.

The Church is ever labouring to make her children holy, not by her teaching only, but by her discipline. "I have written to you," says St Paul, "not to keep company, if any man that is named a brother, be . . . a drunkard: . . . with such an one, not so much as to eat. . . . Put away the evil one from among yourselves" (1 Cor. v. 11–13). We have seen St Augustin discussing questions of discipline—how to reform abuses; how to deal with the incorrigible. In the present chapter we have to inquire into the treatment of drunkenness in later ages and other countries.

It will be asked : What advice was given with regard to combating drunkenness? Was there anything in Catholic antiquity like the modern system of administering the pledge? I reply that we must here distinguish between the substance and the form. If by "administering the pledge" we understand a popular or public enrolment of multitudes in societies, having as their special object to promote sobriety, then it is a novelty in the history of the Church.[1] But if by taking the pledge we mean abstaining from the use of intoxicating drinks, either as a work of perfection, a remedy, or a penance, then it is by no means a novelty, but has been well known in all ages and countries. I can, perhaps, best explain the whole subject by distinguishing the different states and classes of men and women in the Church, and the different purposes for which abstinence was counselled or prescribed.

## DISCIPLINE OF THE CLERGY.

As to the clergy, no synod of any age or country has ever imposed on them total abstinence from fermented liquors. In this the Chris-

[1] Though novel yet not uncatholic, as I shall show in the last chapter, according to the maxim, *Non nova sed nove*.

tian Church is clearly marked off from the Synagogue. Marriage was permitted to Jewish priests, but on the other hand they were forbidden, under pain of death, to taste any intoxicating drink during the time of their service in the tabernacle (Levit. x. 9). The Christian Church has copied the example of her Divine Founder. "Following the Lamb whithersoever He goeth," by a life of celibacy, her priests have been left free like Him to eat meat and to drink wine. No more stringent rule than that of St Paul has been imposed on them. "It behoveth a bishop to be blameless, the husband of one wife,[1] sober, ... not given to wine" (1 Tim. iii. 2, 3). "A bishop must be without crime, ... not given to wine, ... but given to hospitality, gentle, sober" (Tit. i. 7, 8).

Thus what are called the Apostolic Constitutions, which give the discipline of the third century, when exhorting the clergy to sobriety, especially at funerals, add immediately, for fear of being misunderstood: "We say this, not that they are not to drink at all, otherwise it would be the reproach of what God has made

[1] "The meaning is, not that every bishop should have a wife (for St Paul himself had none), but that no one should be admitted to the holy orders of bishop, priest, or deacon, who had been married more than once." Note to the Douay version. From any other interpretation it would follow that other Christians might have more than one wife at once.

for cheerfulness, but that they be not disordered with wine. For the Scripture does not say: Drink not wine;" but what says it? "Drink not wine to drunkenness."[1]

This discipline of the Church may require a few words of explanation. It will surely not be thought that the Church aims at a lower standard than the Synagogue, or expects from her priests less perfection than was required from Jewish priests. As well might it be thought, that Christianity has lower views of morality than Mohammedanism, because the latter requires from its adherents abstinence from intoxicating drinks, while the former does not. We must understand, then, that such abstinence may be either a practice of perfection and a sign of strength, or, on the contrary, a confession of weakness. Among the Jews the abstinence of the Nazarenes was a counsel of perfection; the intermittent abstinence of the priests was a precaution to sustain their infirmity. It has been remarked that the prohibition was issued after the "offering of strange fire in their censers" by Nadab and Abiu (Lev. x. 1-3), whence it has been conjectured that they were tempted to their profanity by the insolence of drink. Be that as it may, the nature of the Jewish priest-

[1] Apost. Const., Book viii. chap. 44 (p. 253, Edinburgh ed. 1870).

hood sufficiently shows the reason of the discipline imposed upon it.

The Levitical priesthood was hereditary. It must have included, therefore, men of every variety of natural temperament and spiritual gifts. Without a perpetual extraordinary providence of God, all its members could not have had the spiritual qualifications befitting the ministry of the Most Holy, and there are no proofs of such a providence. As many were born disqualified, by natural bodily defects, for the service of the tabernacle (see Lev. xxi. 17-23), so must many have been not merely positively unworthy by acquired vices (as may happen even to Christian priests), but also, independently of their own fault and negatively, must have been little qualified for their office. No high standard of perfection could be required from an hereditary priesthood as a body.

An austere life was therefore not prescribed to them. "This shall be the priest's due from the people . . . the first-fruits of corn, of wine, and of oil" (Deut. xviii. 4). "The first-fruits which the children of Israel shall vow and offer, I have given to thee and to thy sons . . . all the best of the oil, and of the wine, and of the corn" (Num. xviii. 11). It is evident that among such men there must have been a perpetual danger of excess, and therefore, during the period when

## Discipline.

the Jewish priests, in the order of their course, took part in the service of the tabernacle, a strict precept of abstinence was imposed on them, "that they might have knowledge to discern between holy and unholy, between unclean and clean" (Lev. x. 10).

The case of the Christian priesthood is quite different. It is not hereditary. No one can enter on it lawfully unless he has both natural and spiritual qualifications, and a distinct divine vocation. Of course, men unqualified may thrust themselves into its ranks, or, again, priests may degenerate from their high vocation and forfeit their spiritual gifts. For such cases special prohibitions may be made, and they may be treated as infirm. But the general legislation of the Church will have regard to the normal state of her clergy. She has a right to expect much of them. As no one is forced into her service, and no one comes in ignorance of her requirements, no one has a right to complain that she exacts too much. She alone, who has the mind of the Spirit, can know what befits the ministry and the weakness of man. From Apostolic times she has adopted, for her clergy in holy orders, the discipline of the perfect, *i.e.*, voluntary celibacy. She may, therefore, treat them as spiritual athletes, and may suppose that men who have vanquished the stronger passions will not be overcome by those which are weaker. She will warn them against danger, and even prohibit what is unbecoming,[1] but while she charges them to be sober, she will leave it to themselves to carry their sobriety into the austerity of total abstinence. That many would do so was certain from the beginning, and has been confirmed by experience. St Timothy, probably copying in this the example of some of the Apostles (for tradition has handed down a similar thing of St James the Just), had made himself a rule to drink only water. Nor did St Paul, as St Chrysostom remarks, advise him to relax this rule until, not one, but frequent infirmities and incessant toil, had made necessary for him a relaxation, which, however slight it might be, it required the authority of an Apostle to induce him to adopt.[2] It would be easy to gather a long list of similar examples from the lives of Christian priests and prelates, among whom I may mention St Boniface and St Anselm. St Jerome, on this subject, wrote to his nephew, the young priest Nepotian:—" Never let the smell of wine

[1] I allude to the prohibitions of entering taverns, etc. How universal such prohibitions have been, may be seen in Dr Smith's Dictionary of Christian Antiquities. Arts. *Drunkenness* and *Caupona*.
[2] See the I. Homily of St. Chrysost. ad Pop. Antioch.

be perceived upon you. . . . Fly from whatever intoxicates. I do not say this as if any creature of God was condemned by us (for we know the charge made against our Lord and the advice given to Timothy); but in respect to drinking we take into account a man's age, health, and strength. If I have already the fire of youth without wine, and am stout and strong, I will gladly forego a drink in which poison may lurk."[1] ' Similar exhortations to the clergy are very frequent.

### Discipline of Ascetics.

As regards monastic bodies, even in the severest rules in which abstinence from flesh-meat was prescribed, I am not aware of any instance of a similar prohibition with regard to all fermented liquors; though I am not prepared to say that such a thing has never been contemplated by the founder of a religious order. Hermits in the mountains and forests must have followed the rule of St John Baptist; but the mode of their penance was adopted by free and individual choice. I need hardly add that multitudes of either sex, though not bound by their monastic rule to total abstinence, have made it the practice of their lives.

[1] S. Hieron. Ep. 52, alias 2.

Blessed Humbert, general of the Dominicans, in the thirteenth century, thus addresses his brethren:[1]—"The Saracens by their law keep perpetual abstinence from wine. The Rechabites in the old law never drank wine, nor the Nazarenes in the time of their consecration. If so much was done in false religions, or in that which was but a figure of ours, how shameful must excess be in a religious man. Many faults may be committed. First in quantity: Therefore St Paul says to St Timothy: 'Use a *little* wine;' and St Bernard: 'If we like so much this authority of the Apostle about drinking wine, at least let us notice the word 'little.'" Secondly, with regard to strength. The Council (of Lateran) says: 'Vinum sibi temperent et se vino.' Thirdly, with regard to variety. It is indecent for religious to use many kinds of wine. One kind is enough. Fourthly, with regard to price, a religious should not in one draught consume what would relieve many poor. The word: 'Let us fill ourselves with costly wine,' was uttered by bad not by good men (Wisdom ii. 7). Fifthly, with regard to time. Even asses are only watered at certain hours. What shall be said of a religious who drinks all day, first here then there? Sixthly, with regard to words. Some talk all dinner time about

[1] Bib. Max. Lugd., tom. xxv. p. 585.

wines, present or absent. Lastly, with regard to judging of wines. Some can judge of the price and qualities of wines as if they had passed master in the art."

The same excellent author gives the following earnest exhortation to such as aspire to an ascetic life :—

"Our rule" (*i.e.* the rule of St Augustin, which St Dominick has adopted) "says: 'Subdue your flesh by fasting and abstinence in food and drink, as far as health permits.' Are then all the professors of this rule bound to mortify the flesh to their utmost power? I reply: There are some things in the rule, which are rather intended as exhortations to what is good, than as strictly preceptive. And such is the above rule. Yet I would observe, that human nature, which was very strong in its original state, is not yet so weakened, but that it can do much in the way of abstinence. This is clearly proved by the great and long abstinence, which men undergo against their wills in prison, or which some undertake to recover their health, and which many saints have practised and still practise, and these not only men but women of delicate constitution. What then could we not do if we loved our souls as much as our bodies? Ah! if men would but try their strength, they would find they could do more than they fancy.

But the shame is, that men try how much they can do in hurling a stone, in running and wrestling, and such things; but in the things of God they do not try their strength. Whence St Bernard cries: 'Pardon us, pardon us, O Lord, we are deceitful and treacherous, and in Thy service no one will try to discover how much he might do.' The sons of Zebedee said that they were able to drink the chalice of the Passion; while *we* cannot bear a slight abstinence. St Paul said: 'I can do all things in Him who strengthens me;' and we, to whom divine help is always offered, distrust our power to do even a few things. Doubtless we could do many, but we will not. 'The cause is not want of power, but the fault is want of will,' says St Jerome."[1]

### DISCIPLINE OF THE LAITY.

The Church of Christ, faithful to her Divine Spouse, has never prohibited what He allowed. She has never enforced celibacy on unwilling populations, as is too often done at the present day in army and workhouse discipline, though she never ceases to repeat His words: Qui potest capere, capiat, "He that can take, let him take it" (Matt. xix. 12). She has never, like

[1] Bib. Max. Lugd., tom. xxv. p. 585.

Mahomet, forbidden by a general law the use of fermented liquors, though she is ever recommending temperance.

On the other hand, the prevalence of error will not induce her to swerve from her principles or her exhortations. When Manichees forbade marriage, the Church did not cease to praise virginity, though her doctors carefully warned the faithful against Manicheean perversity. When Gnostics forbade wine, Clement did not fear to exhort the young to total abstinence, even while proving that our Lord Jesus Christ had Himself drunk wine; and Origen would not suffer those Catholic Christians to be molested, who abstained from intoxicating drinks in order to avoid drunkenness, from any dread lest their motive should be misinterpreted. If St Bernard reproached the Manichees of his day, for "imposing on the people an abstinence of which, for the most part, they are incapable," it is scarcely necessary to say that he is not alluding to such as are willing to embrace abstinence, either as a remedy or as a higher discipline, but of restrictions *imposed* on the multitude beyond the necessary rules of morality. And of course, he is not contemplating the case of abstinence imposed by legitimate authority as a penalty for past transgressions—an abstinence which would be accompanied by a special grace for its observance. In a similar way, we must understand the words of St Gregory the Great, when recommending St Mellitus to deal leniently with the newly-converted English, and to allow them a festival on the dedication of the churches, he remarks :—" They will thus be more easily led from external enjoyments to those of the soul. For there is no doubt that it is impossible to cut away all sensual pleasures at once from *indocile souls*. He who seeks to ascend a height advances by steps, not by jumps."

These saints who would deal so prudently with weak souls, would have been the first to encourage every generous self-sacrifice of individuals or zealous movement of reform among the multitude. Besides this, if feasting was tolerated, fasting was prescribed, and I must here say a few words regarding

## THE FAST OF LENT.

It seems, then, that from the earliest times to deny one's self the use of wine, was looked on as part of the penitential discipline of Lent, both in the East and the West. An important document of the Greek Church in the fourth century, preserved to us by St Jerome,[1] lays down the

[1] S. Hieron., Epist. 100.

following rule : " In seasons of fasting there should be abstinence from flesh and from wine ; the fruits of the earth should be eaten and water drunk." Passages have been already quoted from St Augustin[1] in which he complains of some who, while they denied themselves wine, replaced it by sweet and expensive drinks of other kinds. It is probable that the abstinence did not everywhere include beer. Certainly the monks who, rising at a very early hour, continued fasting until three o'clock in the afternoon, and even later, and who, besides manual labour, spent many long hours in singing the divine office, were allowed a refreshment of beer in common, or of wine where beer was not used. Nor is it easy to discover how long the discipline of the Church enforced abstinence from wine as a Lenten precept. An Anglo-Saxon canon says,[2] " No one should drink to excess in the holy time of Lent. Drunkenness is always prohibited; milk and cheese are not. The apostle did not say, 'Eat no cheese nor eggs,' but, 'Be not drunk with wine (or any other drink), wherein is luxury.'" Here it is the excess, not the simple use that is forbidden ; and

---

[1] See Chap. I.
[2] Wilkins, Concilia, tom. i. pp. 265-282, the 40th canon. These canons seem to be translations of those made by Theodulf of Orleans, in the eighth century.

the canon shows the absurdity of indulging in what is always unlawful while abstaining from what, except for the Church's prohibition, is innocent.

It would seem that abstinence from strong drinks *at* the one meal of Lent (for it was of this that St Jerome and St Augustin wrote), was soon looked on as rather a counsel of perfection than a strict precept. In later ages the maxim has been approved that, while such beverages as milk and broth are forbidden, yet, in general, drink, whether fermented or otherwise, does not fall under the letter of the ecclesiastical law;[1] and may be taken without sin whether at the meal or apart from it. It still remains true, however, that to abstain from fermented liquors at the permitted meal, and much more outside of it, is a counsel of perfection; it is also true that free indulgence in such liquors, even without intoxication, is contrary to the *spirit* of the fast, and may impair or destroy both its natural effects and its supernatural merit; and it is certain that the holy season of Lent adds an aggravating circumstance of guilt to the sin of intoxication. But though the spirit of the Church's penitential discipline remains unchanged, it is evident that the recurrence of Lent exercised a much greater influence on

[1] Liquidum non frangit jejunium.

the Catholic population in former times than it does at present, in restraining the excessive use of fermented liquors. Drunkenness is a vice public by its nature, and it would have much more grievously offended public opinion to have given way to this vice, at a season when the whole population, without exception, was professing the duty of penance and humiliation, than now that the observance of Lent is confined to the few, amidst a vast population which no longer understands the meaning of the word penance, or knows of the existence of a Lenten season. Public opinion, therefore, now exerts little or no influence in this respect on Catholics who are unrestrained by their own conscience; and it would be hard to overrate the loss thus sustained by the nation.

### Treatment of Drunkards.

Those who had become the slaves of intemperance were told to avoid taverns, feasts, the company of drunkards, and other occasions of sin, as also to strengthen themselves against temptation by clear and well-defined resolutions. Our own St Edmund says:—"To overcome gluttony a man ought to fix himself a certain measure of food or drink, but especially of drink."[1]

[1] Speculum Ecclesiæ. Bib. Max. Lugd.

I have sought, however, in vain, among the ancient writers for any careful theological discussion of the treatment of habitual and confirmed drunkards. One of the most explicit passages on this subject is to be found in a sermon of St Cæsarius. These are his words:—" Above all things we ought to understand that men do not become drunkards in a day, but by adding day by day, at the instigation of their most cruel friends, or rather enemies, one or two cups to their usual quantity. But when this has become a habit, drunkenness gets such a hold upon them as to cause them a perpetual longing. But he who desires to be delivered from this evil, just as he reached the darkness of intemperance by adding to his drink day by day, so by diminishing it by degrees let him return to the light of temperance. For if he should retrench suddenly all that he has added (to his former temperate measure), when he begins to feel his burning thirst, he will cry out that he would rather die than give up his habit of drinking to excess. He cares not at that moment about eternal death. So then, that he may not suffer this burning thirst, and that he may be freed from his grievous sin, as I have said, let him gradually, and day by day, retrench somewhat of his excess, until he has returned to a reasonable and moderate manner of drinking."

[1] Sermo 294, in Append., S. Augustini.

This is, of course, only the judgment of a theologian, though of one both holy and experienced. It is not the decision of a council nor the tradition of the Church. The drunkards too, of whom the saint was writing, bad as they were, must not be confounded with the modern victims of ardent spirits, which were then unknown. I would observe also that we must take St Cæsarius's doctrine in connection with the whole system of the Church in his day.

### THE SACRAMENT OF PENANCE.

In Lent and the other fast days, the Church called on all her children, the innocent no less than the guilty, to unite in propitiating the justice of God. But she had, and still has, a special discipline for the guilty. The words of St Gregory the Great are still read in the offices of the Church: "It should be known, that to him who has not done what is unlawful, the law grants the free use of what is innocent. But if any one has fallen into the sin of fornication, or the still more heinous sin of adultery, he ought to deprive himself of what is licit in proportion as he has perpetrated what is illicit. We are told to 'bring forth *worthy* fruits of penance' (Luke iii. 8). But to be worthy, they must not be the same in one who has been less, and in one who has been more guilty, or in one who has fallen into few crimes, and in one who has relapsed into many."[1]

The proportioning of the works of penance to the guilt was not left entirely to the individual conscience, too often a partial judge in its own cause. Nor was it even left to the discretion of every confessor. Even bishops legislated with fear in a matter so difficult and delicate. It was a subject of frequent consultation between the learned and saintly prelates of the principal churches; and the Apostolic traditions and decisions of Synods were looked on as sacred rules, which a local church might modify indeed, according to circumstances of time and place, but might not set aside, and by which the confessor was to be guided, though he also was to consider the circumstances and needs of the individual soul.[2]

We have already heard St Augustin complaining that drunkenness was treated too leniently. The canons called Apostolic had indeed decreed the suspension or degradation

---

[1] Homilia 20 in Evang. lecta Dom. quarta Adventûs.

[2] For a full account of the penitential discipline of the early ages the reader must be referred to the learned treatise of Morinus, or to Chardon's "Histoire des Sacraments," the latter of which, however, is tainted with Jansenism. He may also consult Dr Moran's "Essays on the Early Irish Church" (Dublin, Duffy, 1864).

## Discipline. 71

of the higher clergy (Bishops, Priests, and Deacons), who should be guilty of habitual drunkenness. But in the first ages no special penalty seems to have been appointed for this crime when committed by a layman. Intoxication might of course be a grievous sin, and he who was guilty would have to repent, to confess, and to do penance for it, as at present; but it was not one of the capital crimes for which specific and public penance was imposed; and the very severity with which certain other crimes were punished, such as apostasy, perjury, homicide, and impurity, and the long and public penance to which they were subjected, made the uninstructed think too lightly of a sin which was treated more leniently. Hence we find the early fathers frequently complaining that the grievousness of habitual intemperance was ill understood, and that some who were guilty continued to approach holy communion without purifying themselves by penance.

These complaints and remonstrances caused more attention to be drawn to this vice, especially when it became more frequent after the conversion of the barbarians, and from the sixth century it is treated of in the various penitential codes.

It was a principle in ascetic and penitential discipline that vices should be cured by remedies suited to their nature; and as almsgiving was prescribed to the avaricious, and works of mercy to the proud and cruel, so abstinence from strong drink was appointed as the fit penance for intemperance.

Penal abstinence from strong drink, moreover, entered into the satisfaction exacted for every great crime. So that there were, throughout many centuries of the Church's history, multitudes who, in the performance of the penances imposed on them, abstained from the use of wine or beer one or more days in each week, not only for months, but for years, and even for their whole lives.

Although, in the confusion caused by constant wars and revolutions, many may have neglected for years together to approach the Church's sacraments; and from general ignorance and relaxation of discipline many confessors neglected to enforce the canons; still, on the whole, the tribunal of penance which was established in every hamlet throughout Europe, and frequented by the immense majority at least once a year, cannot but have had a most beneficial and important influence, as in other respects, so also on the sobriety of the people. To the abandonment of this sacrament by so many nations, especially by those of the northern climes most addicted to drunkenness, and to its neglect in other nations owing to indifference and infidelity, must be attributed in no small measure the great prevalence of drunkenness in the last three centuries, and at the present day.

These statements will no doubt be contested by some; and it would enter into the plans of many Protestant temperance reformers to abolish rather than to encourage the frequentation of the sacrament of penance. It is not easy to bring such a question to the test. Many influences are ever at work affecting for good or evil the morality of nations. Natural temperament, soil, climate, riches, war, peace, foreign relations, internal dissensions, discoveries, commerce, means of local communication, and facilities of transport, and above all, good or bad laws, and good or bad administration of laws, all affect the sobriety of a nation as well as religious teaching, sacraments and discipline. It is easy, therefore, to attribute to one cause what is the effect of others; or to overlook a good influence which is neutralised or overpowered by an evil one. We must therefore proceed with caution. I have no wish, in passing judgment on the present day, to impute to the abandonment of "confession" what may be the result of the manufacture of distilled spirits, the multiplication of taverns and public-houses, or the toil and confinement of great factories in our modern civilisation.

On the other hand, if, in spite of the sacrament of penance, we find much drunkenness to have existed in former days, let us have the fairness to consider the frequent invasions, the foreign wars, the mischief arising from the feudal system, and so many other influences at work in past times to disturb society, and to counteract the influence of religion, some of which have now ceased to operate.

Perhaps the surest way to study the action of the Church, and to arrive at some honest conclusions, is to confine our inquiry to one region; and no better region for such a study could be desired than the British Isles. The Church has here had a fair battle-field. She has had to deal with a variety of races, all more or less addicted by nature to intemperance. She has had a long history during which to exercise her powers, and to develop her methods. After many centuries her influences were almost withdrawn from Great Britain, and crippled by persecution in Ireland. We shall be able to see what was the effect of that withdrawal; and whether it was favourable or injurious to the cause of temperance. This then is the investigation which I have pursued, and the results of which I am about to state, in the hope that the history of the past may contain lessons for the present.

# Part the Second.

## THE DOCTRINE AND DISCIPLINE OF THE CHURCH STUDIED IN THEIR RESULTS IN THE BRITISH ISLES.

## CHAPTER IV.

### DRUNKENNESS AN ENGLISH VICE.

IT would certainly be a great exaggeration to assert that drunkenness is a vice peculiar to northern climes. It was frequent among the Jews in the days of the prophets, and was very prevalent in Africa in the time of St Augustin. Still there are countries in which drunkenness is almost unknown. Throughout all the writings of St Peter Damian, which give an appalling picture of Italy in the eleventh century, or those of St Bernardine of Siena in the fifteenth, there is scarcely a passing mention of drunkenness. Nor had the great Italian missionaries of the eighteenth century,

St Leonard of Port Maurice, St Alphonsus de Liguori, or St Paul of the Cross, any need to lift up their voices against it. St Alphonsus has left a sermon which he calls "The Four Gates of Hell." They are Blasphemy, Impurity, Theft, and Hatred. Had the Saint preached in England, Drunkenness would certainly have been a fifth gate, or would have taken the place of Blasphemy.

Nor is drunkenness a vice of modern England merely. Though it has immensely increased in the last two or three centuries with the increase of population and from other causes, yet there has been a tendency, at least amongst the inhabitants of Britain, to the abuse of intoxicating drinks in each successive age with which we are acquainted, and which each invading race has strengthened.

St Gildas, the *Briton*, complains that when peace and abundance were granted to his nation in the fifth century, iniquity everywhere prevailed. "And not only the laity did so," he adds, "but our Lord's own flock and the shepherds who ought to have been an example to the people, slumbered away their time in drunkenness, as if they had been steeped in wine."

As regards the *Teutonic* tribes which succeeded to the Britons, the testimony of St Boniface[1] in

[1] S. Boniface, ep. 70 (ed. Jaffé).

the eighth century is most explicit. Writing to Cuthbert, Archbishop of Canterbury, from Germany, he says :—" It is reported that in your dioceses the vice of drunkenness is too frequent ; so that not only certain bishops do not hinder it, but they themselves indulge in excess of drink, and force others to drink till they are intoxicated. This is most certainly a great crime for a servant of God to do or to have done, since the ancient canons decree that a bishop or a priest given to drink should either resign or be deposed. And Truth itself has said:—'Take heed to yourselves lest perhaps your hearts be overcharged with surfeiting and drunkenness' (Luke xxi. 34), and St Paul, 'Be not drunk with wine wherein is luxury' (Eph. v. 18) ; and the prophet Isaias, 'Woe to you that are mighty to drink wine, and stout men at drunkenness' (Is. v. 22).

"This is an evil peculiar to pagans and to our race (nostræ gentis). Neither the Franks, nor the Gauls, nor the Lombards, nor the Romans, nor the Greeks commit it.

"Let us then repress this iniquity by decrees of Synods and the prohibitions of the Scriptures if we are able. If we fail, at least by avoiding and denouncing it, let us clear our own souls from the blood of the reprobate."

The invasion of the *Danes* only added to the evil. "There was scarcely a village in England," says Brompton, "in which Danes were not dwelling with the English. But by nature the Danes are mighty drinkers, and this quality they have left as a perpetual inheritance to the English. King Edgar, therefore, had pegs fixed in the bowls that they might drink by measure."

We shall consider the nature and value of this effort to check drunkenness presently. It was not very efficacious, according to William of Malmesbury,[1] who attributes the easy conquest of the English by the Normans, especially to the prevailing habits of intemperance. "Public drinking was the custom of all classes; and day and night was spent in such potations." He adds that they communicated these habits to their conquerors.

Certainly the mixture of *Norman* blood, if it did not increase, did not much mitigate the evil. John of Salisbury, towards the close of the twelfth century, writing to his friend, Peter of Celles,[2] says:—"You know that habits of drinking (potationis assiduitas) have made the English famous among all foreign nations;" and in another letter,[3] written from France to a friend in England—"Both nature and national customs

---

[1] Willel. Mal. Gesta Reg., Ang. Lib. iii. 418 (ed. Hardy). Patrol. tom. 179, col. 1229 (ed. Migne).
[2] Joannes Sarisbur, ep. 85. Bib. Max. Lugd., tom 23.
[3] Ibid., ep. 266.

make you drunkards. It is a strife between Ceres and Bacchus. But in the beer which conquers and reigns and domineers with you, Ceres prevails."

That the English, as John of Salisbury says, were famous for their drinking propensities, is curiously proved by a saying reported of Pope Innocent III. in 1206. When the case of the exemption of the Abbey of Evesham from the Bishop of Worcester was being argued before the Roman Pontiff, the Bishop's advocate said :— " Holy Father, we have learnt in the schools, and this is the opinion of our masters, that there is no prescription against the rights of bishops." The Pope replied :—" Certainly, both you and your masters had drunk too much English beer when you learnt this."

Innocent had met many English scholars and masters when he studied in Paris, and he may have spoken from experience.

What now are we to say about *Ireland?*

Giraldus Cambrensis or Gerald Barry, Archdeacon of Brecknock (1175–1200), after extolling the constant fasting and zealous preaching of the Irish clergy, and their scrupulous observance of chastity, thus concludes : [2]—" Among so many thousands you will not find one who, after

---

[1] Chronicon Abbat. de Evesham, p. 189. (Rolls ed.)
[2] Top. d. 3, lib. 27.

all his vigorous observance of fasts and prayer, will not make up at night for the labours of the day, by drinking wine and other liquors beyond all bounds of decorum." It is evident, of course, at first sight that here there must be exaggeration. We have, indeed, instances enough in the false religions of Brahminism and Mohammedanism of the union of corporal austerities of a certain kind with great sensual indulgence. But it is simply impossible that men should be rigorous in fasting, scrupulous in purity, zealous in prayer and preaching, and yet habitually indulge in excess of drink. There must be mistake or misrepresentation, and Giraldus is so reckless in other statements that his words have little authority here. Dr Lynch, in his Cambrensis Eversus,[1] shows that we may receive Barry's testimony to the publicly edifying life of the clergy, but that the assertion that they compensated at night and in secret is too like the malicious suspicions indulged by those who are incapable of believing in virtue, to merit any attention. Barry could not know it of his own experience, and has clearly generalised in an outrageous manner—("scarce one among so many thousands")—the gossip of sneering enemies. Dr Lynch also remarks that St Lawrence O'Toole, while severe in chastising other

[1] Vol. iii. ch. 31, p. 353 (ed. Kelly).

vices of the clergy, is not recorded to have had occasion to punish that of intemperance.

In the year 1186, Barry again extolled the chastity and abstinence of the clergy, adding that it was a miracle that where wine held sway Venus also should not reign. Dr Lanigan, however, will by no means admit the possibility of such a miracle, and holds that the acknowledged chastity overthrows the accusation of intemperance. He thus explains the origin of Barry's misrepresentation :—" Not being able to show that the clergy drank to excess, he strove to misrepresent the practice of the country, as if it were more unbecoming to drink something after dinner than to drink as much as people do in some other countries during their long dinners."[1]

I must leave this controversy to the reader's judgment, merely remarking that it is hard to get at historical truth where questions of nationality are involved. It is, however, fair to add that the English martyr Campion, who wrote his account of Ireland in 1571, though he speaks of the immoderate use of aqua vitæ by the soldiers in Ireland, yet lays no charge of drunkenness on the nation. It is still more remarkable that the poet Spencer, who, in his view of Ireland, is excessively severe in speaking of

[1] History of the Irish Church, lib. iv. c. 30, p. 268.

Irish vices, does not mention love of strong drinks among the number.

I have read through a MS. Visitation Book of the Archdiocese of Cashel, made during two or three years in the middle of the last century, in which are detailed reports from each parish on the moral condition of the people, and every fault requiring correction is mentioned, but the vice of drunkenness scarcely occurs. On the other hand, in the Life of Archbishop Plunket, who was martyred in 1681, we find that drunkenness was one of the principal evils he was called on to correct in the North.[1] On the whole, the evidence would seem to prove that drunkenness as a national vice in Ireland is of a very modern date.

[1] His account of this will be given in Chapter X.

# CHAPTER V.

#### DRINKS USED IN FORMER TIMES.

 CURIOUS document lately brought to light would seem to show, that in the 15th century at least, water was looked upon as an unwholesome drink in England. The Spanish Ambassador at the court of Henry VII., De Puebla Talavera, writes to Ferdinand and Isabella, 17th July 1498, that the English Queen, and Lady Margaret, the King's mother, wish that the young princess Katharine of Arragon, being affianced to the Prince of Wales (though still living in Spain), " should accustom herself to drink wine, since the water in England is not drinkable, and even if it were, the climate would not allow the drinking of it."[1] In the same century Sir

---

[1] Bergenroth's Calendar of State Papers, l. 156, quoted by Mr Mayor in his ed. of Cooper's Life of Lady Margaret, p. 231.

John Fortescue boasted, perhaps a little hyperbolically, that the English never drank water except as a penance.

On the other hand, if we may credit an old poet,[1] no other kind of drink was unwelcome to the English taste :—

> "The Russ drinks quass; Dutch Lubeck beer,
>   And that is strong and mighty;
> The Briton,[2] he metheglin quaffs,
>   The Irish aqua vitæ;
> The French affects the Orleans grape,
>   The Spaniard tastes his sherry;
> The English none of these can 'scape,
>   But he with all makes merry."

It is not necessary for my purpose to inquire minutely into the composition or history of the various strong drinks used by our forefathers. A few particulars, however, which I have noted, may not, perhaps, be without interest, at least to the unlearned.

## 1. Beer and Ale.

"All the nations who inhabit the west of Europe," says Pliny, "have a liquor with which they intoxicate themselves, made of corn and water."[3] This liquor was well known in Britain

---

[1] Heywood's Rape of Lucrece. (Percy Society.)
[2] *I.e.* the Welshman.   [3] Hist. Nat. l. 14, c. 22.

## Ancient Drinks. 85

before the Saxons brought it from the continent. Hearne, the antiquary, in the preface to the "Curious Discourses," discourses very curiously on the national predilection for *beer*. After quoting Athanæus to the effect that malt liquor was called βρυτον, he adds:[1] "which being so, it is humbly offered to the consideration of more judicious persons, whether our Britannia might not be denominated from Bruton, the whole nation being famous for such a sort of drink."

In the genealogy of Jestyn, the son of Gwrgan, it is said: "Ceraint the drunkard was the first who made malt liquor properly; and the commencement was thus:—After he had boiled the wort, together with field flowers and honey, a boar came there, and drinking of it cast in his foam, which caused the liquor to ferment. The beer thus prepared was superior to any ever known before, and thence arose the practice of putting barm in wort. Having attained this knowledge, Ceraint gave himself up entirely to drunkenness, in which state he died."[2]

I do not know the date of this worthy, and the whole history is probably a fable; yet

---

[1] Quoted by Rev. W. Macray in his Preface to the Chronicon de Evesham, p. 25 (Rolls ed).
[2] Published in 1848 by the Welsh MS. Society, p. 339.

Welsh ale is often mentioned in Anglo-Saxon charters as a "sweet ale," and distinguished from "mild ale," and "bright ale."[1] It is not necessary to discuss the difference between beer and ale or the different kinds of each. England has always been famous for its beer and ale. William Fitz-Stephen, in his life of St Thomas of Canterbury, relates[2] that when he went as chancellor into France to negotiate a royal marriage, "two of the waggons which accompanied him were laden with beer in iron-bound casks for presents to the French, who admire that kind of drink, for it is wholesome, clear, of the colour of wine, and of a better taste."

However there was thick beer also, which a Norman poet of the time of Henry III. compares to a Stygian marsh; and of which he makes rather rude fun.[3] There was also weak as well as strong beer. Matthew Paris, in his Life of John, the 23d Abbot of St Albans (c. A.D. 1250), praises him because he increased the strength of the beer, "which to our loss and disgrace was till then very weak." It must be remembered, however, that besides its hundred monks and large body of re-

[1] See Kemble, Saxons in England, vol. i. p. 315.
[2] Migne Patrol. Lat. tom. 190, p. 120.
[3] Henry of Avranches, quoted by Camden, Britannia p. 554 (ed. 1753).

# Ancient Drinks. 87

tainers, the abbey had a constant hospitality to dispense to kings, bishops, and nobles, and also doles of bread and beer to the poor, of which mention is often made in the annals.

The prices of beer and ale varied from two or even three or four gallons for a penny in 1266, to one quart for a penny in 1604, as the price was settled by Acts of Parliament, or by local assize.

## 2. MEAD.

Mead, metheglin, or hydromel, is a strong drink produced by the fermentation of honey mixed with water, and flavoured by herbs or spices. It was more used than wine by the old English; but we have no means of ascertaining the extent of its manufacture. It was an article of excise in the time of Charles II., but is very little known at the present day.

## 3. WINE.

In a Saxon colloquy, quoted by Mr Turner,[1] the youth who is asked what he drinks, replies: "Ale if I have it, or water if I have it not." Being questioned why he does not drink wine, says: "I am not so rich that I can buy me

[1] History of the Manners of the Anglo-Saxons, p. 68.

wine, and wine is not the drink of children, but of the elders and the wise."

Wine is not a natural product of our climate. Tacitus remarks[1] that the Romans found England fit for the cultivation of all kind of fruit-trees except the vine and the olive. Yet they obtained from the Emperor Probus leave to plant vines and to make wine in England, about A.D. 278. We know from monastic chronicles and from charters,[2] that the vine continued to be cultivated in the southern and midland counties of England, until the union with England of the wine-growing districts of France made it unnecessary.

But wine has been imported into England from the very earliest times. It was abundant, as St Gildas testifies, before the invasion of the Saxons, probably imported from France and Italy. Wine was also a common drink of the Saxon nobles, but we have very little knowledge of the quantities or the qualities of the wines sold in England before the Conquest.

Luxury had reached a great height in the twelfth century. "I remember," writes John of

[1] Tacitus. Agricola.
[2] On this subject see Sir H. Ellis's Introduction to Domesday-Book, or Henderson's History of Ancient and Modern Wines. Interesting details will be found in Mr Webb's Illustrations of Bishop Swinfield's Roll, pp. xliii.-xlvii. (Camden Society, 1855.)

Salisbury,[1] "that I was once a guest at the supper of a rich man in Apulia. It lasted from the ninth hour of the day (perhaps 3 P.M.) to midnight. Our host had brought together delicacies from Constantinople, from Babylon, from Alexandria, from Palestine, from Tripoli, Barbary, Syria, and Phœnicia; just as if Sicily, Calabria, Apulia, and Campania were not sufficient to provide a sumptuous banquet." These extravagances were no doubt one of the results of the Crusades. But the union of the wine-growing districts of France with the English crown, by the accession of the Plantagenets, made wine far more plentiful in England than it had ever been before; and according to the expression of a monastic chronicler writing of the year 1200, the first of King John "filled England with drink and drinkers."[2]

From this time wine became so important an article of commerce as to call for much legislation, as we shall see in a subsequent chapter.

From the Exchequer rolls it appears that in 1272 about nine thousand tuns of wine paid duty. A century later, in 1372, according to Froissart, there arrived at the port of Bordeaux

---

[1] De Nugis Curialium Lib. viii. cap. 7, a book filled with curious learning of classical antiquity, as well as details of the manners of the twelfth century.

[2] Repleta est terra potu et potatoribus. Burton Annals.

from England "a fleet of not less than two hundred sail of merchantmen coming for wines."

But wine was imported not only from the west coast of France, but from many other regions. "In the earlier days of the Plantagenets, says Mr Riley,[1] if not at a still more remote period, a wine fleet, its fright probably of the banks of the Moselle, was in the habit of visiting this country every year." Italian, Sicilian, Greek, and Spanish wines were also in great request. The red wines were the produce of Gascony, that is of Poitou and Guienne, and the whole of the district between the Loire and the Pyrenees. "Claret," or "vin clairet," was a more delicate species of a pale red colour. White wines were both French and Rhenish. Sweet wines were sometimes natural growths such as Muscadelle and the famous Malmsey, or Malvoisie, which was a Greek wine obtained from Candia by means of the Venetians; sometimes they were harsh and acid wines sweetened by the mixture of honey and sugar and spices. These were called Piments.[2] The most famous kinds of Piments are mentioned by Chaucer—

"He drinketh Ipocras, Clarrie, and Vernage
Of spices hote, to encrease his corage."[3]

---

[1] Introduction to the Munimenta Gildhallæ, vol. ii., p. 36.
[2] From Pigmentum.   [3] Merchant's Tale.

The same poet thus wittily describes the strength of the Spanish wines:—

> "Now kepe you fro the white and fro the red:
> Namely from the white wine of Lepe,[1]
> That is to sell in Fish-street and in Chepe;
> This wine of Spain crepeth subtelly,
> And other wines groweth fast by,
> Of which riseth such fumosite
> That when a man hath drunk draughts thre,
> And weneth that he be at home in Chepe
> He is in Spain, right at the town of Lepe."[2]

The slight account here given of the wine consumption in England in former days will be sufficient for my purpose, which is to indicate as fairly as I can what was the extent of the evil or the danger with which the Church had then to cope. To form a correct judgment on this point it should be remembered that the arts of adulteration were then but little known. Wines and ales were pure, and therefore more healthy and less intoxicating than at present. "A quantity of alcohol," it is said,[3] "forming an integral portion of some good sound wine, will not affect the head to the extent, or with the rapidity, that half the quantity will do when taken pure, or still more rapidly when diluted with water." The same author adds that "the pure light wines of France and Germany pro-

---

[1] Lepe, now Niebla, a port near Seville. It seems the sacks (vino secco) or dry wines were principally Spanish.
[2] Pardoner's Tale.    [3] Penny Cyclopædia, art. wine.

duce an agreeable exhilaration of mind very unlike the mere physical excitement, almost amounting to ferocity, which results from the largely brandied wines which are too much the vogue in England."

But the wines drunk by our forefathers, if not always unsophisticated, were at least not mingled with distilled spirits, much less were these used as a popular beverage. Yet a few words, at least, must be devoted to them.

## 4. Spirits.

The distillation of aqua vitæ was already known in the thirteenth century or earlier; but until about the sixteenth century the use of distilled spirits was almost confined to experiments in alchemy. In the time of Henry VIII., however, Irish aqua vitæ or usquebaugh had acquired a reputation in England, and Irish distillers were brought into Pembrokeshire. Moryson, writing of the end of the sixteenth century, says:—" At Dublin, and in some other cities, they have taverns wherein Spanish and French wines are sold, but more commonly the merchants sell them by pints and quarts in their own cellars. The usquebaugh is preferred before our (*i.e.*, the English) aqua vitæ, because the mingling of raisins, fennel seeds, and other things, mitigating the heat and making the taste pleasant, makes it less inflame. These drinks the English-Irish drink largely, and in many families both men and women use excess therein; but when they come to any market town to sell a car or horse, they never return home till they have drank the price in Spanish wine, which they call the King of Spain's daughter."[1]

This passage acquaints us with the kind of spirits then used in Ireland. But at the period when Moryson wrote, the consumption had received a great check. An Act of the Irish Parliament had been passed in the 3d of Philip and Mary (A.D. 1556), the preamble of which is as follows:—" Forasmuch as aqua vitæ, *a drink nothing profitable to be daily drunken and used*, is now universally throughout the realm made, and thereby much corn, grain, and other things consumed, spent, and wasted, to the great hindrance, cost, and damage of the poor inhabitants of this realm," &c. This Act prohibits the manufacture of aqua vitæ, without the Lord Deputy's licence, except by peers, gentlemen of £10 freehold, and freemen for their private use. It was not till the beginning of the eighteenth century that distillation was encouraged in Ireland. Heywood, therefore, might be justified in singing of the national predilection for aqua

[1] Fynes Moryson, quoted by Dr Lees, p. 39.

vitæ, without intending thereby to say that the liquor was very common among the peasantry. That it was not a popular drink till a much later period seems to be generally admitted.

Campion, who was in Ireland in 1571, speaks of spirits as the drink of the rude and brutal soldiers, whom he describes as "swilling aqua vitæ after a surfeit of half-raw meat, by quarts and pottles;"[1] but he nowhere mentions it as a national beverage.

It does not seem, indeed, to have got at that time among the peasantry—for Spencer, in his "Views of the State of Ireland," describing the insolence of the soldiers (not all Irish of course), writes:[2]—"The soldiers during their lying at cess (*i.e.*, when billeted on householders) use all kinds of outrageous disorder and villany, both towards the poor men which victual and lodge them, as also to all the country round about them, whom they abuse, oppress, spoil, and afflict by all means they can invent; for they will not only not content themselves with such victuals as their hosts, nor yet as the place perhaps affords, but they will have other meat provided for them, and aqua vitæ sent for, yea and money besides, laid at their trenches."

[1] History of Ireland, by Edmund Campion, p. 25 (ed. Ware, 1809).
[2] View of State of Ireland, p. 132 (ed. Ware, 1809).

## Ancient Drinks.

This passage seems to prove that aqua vitæ was at that time a well-known but somewhat rare drink.

An account of Ireland, written by a Spaniard who had spent some months there in 1579, was presented by him to the Holy See. He says:—
"If you except the seaport towns, there are no hotels or lodging-houses to be found in the island. Every traveller sets up in the first house he meets, and is there provided with whatsoever he desires, gratuitously. Table is not usually laid until evening, but in the meantime drink is not denied to travellers. There are eight sorts of draughts, beer made of barley and water, milk, whey, wine, broth, mead, usquebagh, and spring water."[1] Campion, in the work above referred to, says:—"The Irish drink whey, milk, and beef-broth."

As regards Scotland, I suppose a distinction would have to be drawn between the Highlands and the Lowlands.

Sir Walter Scott is indeed only painting an imaginary Highland festival in his novel "The Fair Maid of Perth," yet he may be supposed to be well informed on such a subject. He is writing of the year 1396: "Even the liquor

---

[1] Quoted from the original MS. by Dr Moran in his History of the Catholic Archbishops of Dublin, vol. i. p. 91.
[2] Ch. xxviii.

itself," he says, "did not seem to raise the festive party above the tone of decorous gravity. It was of various kinds. Wine appeared in very small quantities, and was served out only to the principal guests. Distilled liquors, since so generally used in the Highlands, were then comparatively unknown. The usquebaugh was circulated in small quantities, and was highly flavoured with a decoction of saffron and other herbs, so as to resemble a medicinal potion rather than a festive cordial. Cider and mead were seen at the entertainment; but ale, brewed in great quantities for the purpose, and flowing round without any restriction, was the liquor generally used, and that was drunk with a moderation much less known among the more modern Highlanders."

Wine was, of course, far more plentiful in the Lowlands. Dunbar, writing in 1500, invites his friend—

> "To drink with us the new fresh wine
> That grew upon the river Rhine;
> Fresh fragrant clarets out of France,
> Of Angiers, and of Orleans."

And Dunbar's editor, Mr Paterson, tells us:[1]— "In ancient times, from our intimate connection with France, wine was abundant and cheap in

[1] Life and Poems of William Dunbar, by James Paterson, p. 93.

Scotland, and great care was taken that it should not be adulterated. In 1482 it was enacted by Parliament that those who mixed or corrupted wine should be punished by death.

"Ale and wine were the chief drinks in old times. Usquebaugh, or whisky, is never mentioned in any of the writings of the fifteenth and sixteenth centuries, at least in so far as we have seen. If distilled in the Highlands at that period, which is very doubtful, it must have been gradually brought into repute as the taxes on foreign liquors were increased; and yet we know that the making of corn-brandy, a species of whisky, has been long practised by the Scandinavians."

5. It only concerns my present purpose to speak of intoxicating drinks. In estimating the extent of their use it is, however, necessary to reflect what unintoxicating drinks there were to put in competition with them. In spite of the testimony of the court of Henry VII., I have no doubt that water was pure and harmless. Milk was abundant. Whey, buttermilk, and broth were at hand. Tea, coffee, chocolate were of course unknown. Yet that there were some pleasant artificial drinks known to those who made a profession of abstaining from what might intoxicate, is clearly proved by a passage of a

writer of the fifth century. "Those who refuse themselves wine," he writes,[1] "and then flood themselves with divers other drinks, do not appear to be temperate. Perhaps they abstain from wine for the praise of men, and compensate their abstinence by sweet and pleasant liquors." The writer does not tell us how these liquors were composed, but it would seem that it was not left to Mohammedans to invent sherbet or lemonade, or whatever were the unintoxicating drinks alluded to.

But having seen what means our ancestors possessed wherewith to intoxicate themselves if they were so minded, we must next ascertain what were the social customs involving the use of these means, since much of the drunkenness in every age is rather the result of social habits than of solitary and deliberate indulgence.

[1] De Vita Contemplativa, lib. ii. cap. 12.

## CHAPTER VI.

### DRINKING CUSTOMS.

IN the following notes on the drinking customs of our ancestors, I am rather the historian than the moralist. Some things may have been perfectly innocent, others clearly bad, and others only dangerous or liable to abuse. We shall see in another chapter what the Church thought of these things and how she treated them.

1. FEASTING of course belongs to all ages and all nations, and a plentiful supply of strong drink, a greater variety, a superior excellence, have always been considered as almost essential to a feast. A convivium is also a symposium. The English have never departed from these primitive views.

In the old Anglo-Saxon poem of " Judith," the description of the revels of Holofernes is clearly drawn, not from Asian, but from native sources. The following is Mr Thorpe's translation:—

"There were deep bowls
Carried along the benches often;
So likewise cups and pitchers
Full, to the people who were sitting on couches,
The renowned shielded warriors
Were fated, while they partook thereof.
Then was Holofernes,
The munificent patron of men,
In the guest hall.
He laughed and rioted,
Made tumult and noise,
That the children of men
Might hear afar
How the stern one
Stormed and shouted;
Moody and drunk with mead,
Exhorted abundantly
The sitters on the bench,
So that they conducted themselves well." [1]

There is but too much evidence that the frantic revels in which our pagan forefathers placed the main joy of life, next to fighting, were by no means abandoned after the conversion of the nation to Christianity, though they were no longer so universal nor perhaps so wild in their excess.

The Normans were more refined in their entertainments than the Saxons, perhaps more luxurious, but less prone to gross indulgence. John of Salisbury, writing in the twelfth century, in his great work, "De Nugis Curialium," has two or three chapters about feasting.[2] He

[1] Thorpe's Analecta Anglo-Saxonica.
[2] Book viii. ch. vi.-x.

distinguishes between vulgar feasts, "when the mightiest tippler is considered the best man," and polite feasts, "where sobriety becomes joyous and plenty does not lead to excess." Quoting from Virgil the account of Dido's entertainment of Æneas, he remarks that Christians may learn something even from pagans. It was with pious intention that the feast was begun by the invocation of the gods; although, he adds cautiously, when God is called to preside over a banquet, both immoderate eating and drinking and unseemly talk must be put aside, " for either God is not Himself temperate, or intemperance must displease Him." He remarks also how Iopas sings, at the banquet, of the sun, moon, and the course of nature; and exclaims, " Would that among Christians were heard nothing worse than what the long-haired and rude Iopas sang at the luxurious feast of Dido! Would that foolish and immodest love-songs were banished from the houses of the wise, and that what is sung might either edify, or at least please without corrupting."

In the next chapter, he gives the history of sumptuary laws among the ancient Romans and examples of their luxury. After relating how ancient Rome brought and adopted the tutelary gods of every nation, he says that England does the same with regard to the delicacies of every nation.[1] "When William the Conqueror had established peace in England, he sent messengers into foreign nations that they might find out and bring hither whatever was magnificent or wonderful in each country. Hence there flowed into our opulent island—which is almost able to supply its wants with its own productions—every kind of splendour and of luxury. It was no doubt a praiseworthy ambition in that great man to provide his own subjects with whatever was excellent in other nations; yet he would have deserved more renown, had he rather promulgated laws of temperance to a nation, which he would not have subdued by arms, had it not been already conquered by excess of luxury."

William of Malmesbury, with regard to this very period, relates the following anecdote of St Wulstan, who was appointed Bishop of Worcester by St Edward. "In the time of William the Conqueror, he was obliged to maintain a large retinue of men-at-arms, since the Danes were daily expected. He would not dine in private, but sat down in his public hall with his boisterous soldiers; and while they sat drinking for

---

[1] This saying was reversed by Talleyrand. He remarked that the English have but one sauce (melted butter) and a hundred religions, while the French have a hundred sauces but only one religion.

hours together after dinner, according to the English fashion, he would keep them company to restrain them by his presence, pledging them when it came to his turn in a tiny cup, which he pretended to taste, and in the midst of the din ruminating to himself on the psalms."

A device of another kind is related of St Margaret in her attempts to civilise the rude barons of her husband's court. She persuaded the courtiers to remain till grace was said after dinner, by giving to those who remained a cup of choicer wine. Both these saints were singularly austere in their own lives.

2. Intimately connected with feasts is the custom of PLEDGES, which under one form or another has prevailed in every country. The story told by Geoffrey of Monmouth[1] may or may not be historically true, yet it incorporates an undoubted custom of the Welsh.

"Vortigern the king," he says, writing of the fifth century, "was entertained by his Saxon ally Hengist at a banquet, and when that was over the Lady Rowena, Hengist's daughter, came out of her chamber, bearing a golden cup of wine, with which she approached the king, and, making a low courtesy, said to him, 'Laverd king wacht heil!' The king, at the sight of the lady's face, was on a sudden both sur-

[1] British History, book vi. ch. xi., Thompson's translation.

prised and inflamed with her beauty, and calling to his interpreter asked him what she said, and what answer he should make her. 'She called you Royal Lord,' said the interpreter, 'and offered to drink your health. Your answer to her must be, Drinc heil.' Vortigern accordingly answered, 'Drinc heil,' and bade her drink, after which he took the cup from her hand, kissed her, and drank himself. From that time to this," continues Geoffrey, "it has been the custom in Britain that he who drinks to any one says, 'Wacht heil!' and he that pledges him answers, 'Drinc heil.' Vortigern being now drunk with the variety of liquors, the devil took this opportunity to enter into his heart, and to make him in love with the damsel, so that he became suitor to her father for her. It was, I say, by the devil's entering into his heart that he who was a Christian should fall in love with a pagan. By this example Hengist, being a prudent man, discovered the king's levity, and consulted with his brother Horsa and the other ancient men present what to do in relation to the king's request. They unanimously advised him to give him his daughter, and in consideration of her to demand the province of Kent."

3. Closely connected again with pledging was the practice of CHALLENGING or provoking to drink, whether from perverted notions of hospi-

tality or a still more perverse spirit of emulation. Perhaps there is no more fruitful source of drunkenness at the present day than the custom of pressing, or still more of mutual treating. To put some measure to this practice, which seems to have prevailed especially where the Danes and the English lived together, King Edgar,[1] by the advice of St Dunstan, had pegs or pins put in the bowls, sometimes of silver or gold. No one at a draught might drink below his peg, or compel another to do so. But, on the other hand, it became a fashion that no one should stop short of his limit. We shall see St Anselm legislating on this custom.

4. WAKES, which were another occasion of drinking, were of two sorts—the wakes of the saints, and the wakes of the dead.

As regards the first an old homily says, "Ye shall understand and know how the Evens were first found in old time. In the beginning of Holy Church, it was so that the people came to the church with candles burning, and would wake and come with light towards night to the church in their devotions, and after, they fell to songs, dances, and harping and piping, and also to gluttony and sin, and so turned the holiness to cursedness. Wherefore holy fathers ordained

---

[1] Wilhelm Malmesb., Gesta Reg.-Angl., lib. ii. 237 (ed. Hardy).

the people to leave that waking, and to fast the even. But it is called Vigilia, that is, waking in English; and it is called the Even, for at even they are wont to come to the church." As this custom was especially observed on the eve of the saint to whom the church was dedicated, the name of wake is still given to the church feast. In Ireland it is called a "patern"—*i.e.*, a patron-feast.

The custom of waking the dead—that is, of watching round the dead body in prayer—also degenerated in course of time into a carousal, as hospitality prompted the friends of the deceased to give refreshment to the watchers.

We shall see the Church legislating against both these abuses.

5. But what caused the Church a still harder and more lasting struggle was the custom of celebrating ALES.

Ben Jonson, in his "Tale of a Tub," invites his readers or hearers to leave

> "Wakes and ales
> And old wives' tales,"

for more courtly scenes; and I, on the contrary, must invite my reader to endeavour to transport himself in spirit back to the "wakes and ales" of our forefathers. An ale is a very English institution. It means a gathering of persons by appointment to drink ale, generally

## Drinking Customs. 107

with some farther object in view. The word Scotallum in our English councils has often and naturally puzzled foreign students. It is an attempt to make Latin out of the very English word Scot-ale. *Scot* means payment, or that which is *cast* down in payment. Scot-free means having to pay nothing for one's entertainment. A scot-ale therefore was a meeting where each of the company paid for his share of the drink. In law it is " the keeping of an alehouse by the officer of a forest, and drawing people to spend their money for fear of his displeasure;"[1] but though this definition may cover the use of the word in the old civil law, it had a wider popular use, and stands in our old canon law for all public potations. We find that drinking assemblies were used as convenient means of raising money. Either the profits derived from the sale of the drink, or subscriptions made when the heart was warmed with the ale, were devoted to the purpose in hand.

A *Bid-ale*, when any man decayed in his estate was set up again by the contributions of his friends at a feast, to which those friends were *bid*den or invited. It was much used in the

[1] Ogilvie's Imperial Dictionary.

West of England, and in some counties called a *help-ale*.

In some of the large towns of Yorkshire at the present day "a barrel-of-beer-stir" answers the same purpose. The friends of a poor widow, for example, or of a person wishing to emigrate, will buy a barrel of beer. The time for drinking this is announced, and the friends meet, the men paying a shilling, the women sixpence, and the profits are given to the charity.

A *Bride-ale*, says Brande,[1] Bride-bush, Bride-stake are nearly synonymous terms, and all derived from the circumstance of the bride's selling ale on the wedding-day, for which she received by way of contribution whatever handsome price the friends assembled on the occasion chose to pay her for it. A bush at the end of a stake or pile was the ancient badge of a country ale-house. Around the stake the guests were wont to dance as about a Maypole. The bride-ale appears in some places to have been called a bidding, from the circumstance of the bride and bridegroom bidding or inviting the guests. In Cumberland it had the appellation of a bride's wain."[2]

---

[1] Popular Antiquities, vol. ii. p. 70.
[2] I find *Dove-Ale* also mentioned in a Lancashire document of the year 1590 (Chetham Miscellanies, vol. v.). I do not know its nature.

A *Give-ale* was the name sometimes applied to the doles of bread and ale which were very commonly distributed at the funerals or month's mind, or annual obits of rich men.

Thus early in the ninth century Oswulf, a duke in Kent, devised[1] lands to Christ Church, Canterbury, which he charged with annual doles to the poor on his anniversary. "Forty hides at Stanhampstead were to find 120 loaves of wheat, 30 loaves of fine wheat, one fat ox or four sheep, two flitches of bacon, five geese, ten hens, and ten pounds of cheese. Moreover, thirty ambers of good Welsh ale, on the footing of fifteen *mittan*, and one *mitta* of honey" (perhaps to make into a drink), "or two of wine." Fabyan[2] tells us that Robert Chichely, grocer, who had been twice Lord Mayor of London, by his will in 1438, ordained that upon his mind-day a good and competent dinner should be provided for 2400 poor men, householders of the city if possible. The worthy chronicler himself made due provision for bread, meat, cheese, and ale to be distributed at his funeral and at his month's mind. But there are few wills of wealthy nobles or citizens without clauses to the same effect.

Not quite so praiseworthy, though still innocent enough, are the legacies made to the rich

[1] Quoted by Kemble in his Saxons in England, vol. i. p. 315.
[2] Chronicle, p. 616 (ed. Ellis).

assistants at funerals. Katharine Cooke,[1] widow of John Cooke, sometime Mayor of Cambridge, dying in 1496, left fifteen pence in money "to the mayor, bailiffs, and such of their brethren there being present at the said dirge, at the calling of the said mayor and bailiffs, to the tavern for a solace there among them to be had." John Keynsham,[2] alderman of Cambridge in 1502, appointed by his will an obit, at which the mayor, bailiffs, &c., shall assist, and that immediately after the dirge "a recreation, otherwise called a junkett or banquet, to be had within the Abbey of Barnewell, at cost and charge of the treasurers, at which to be spent six shillings and eightpence in bread, cheese, a hogget of good ale and another of hostel ale;" for which he leaves foundation.

Such sums, though we might multiply them by twelve or twenty for modern value, would provide no very dangerous carouse, and the custom could be only hurtful if such foundations or bequests became frequent. As, however, they were all connected with the celebration of the Requiem Mass, they ceased with the Reformation under Edward. In the time of Henry, a reformer named Fish had written his "Supplication of Beggars," asking that the money left to

[1] Cooper's Annals of Cambridge, vol. i. p. 246.
[2] Ibid., p. 259.

## Drinking Customs.

the clergy might be taken from them for the relief of the poor. Sir Thomas More had written a reply called "The Supplication of Souls," putting forward the claims of the souls in purgatory. But it was so managed under Edward, that both the souls and the poor lost their legacies, and yet the State was none the richer.

But the custom of ales was not confined to secular objects, or even to charity to the poor. It was often a parochial institution, and was called a *church-ale*; and was used as an easy means of supporting the fabric of the church or procuring its necessary ornaments. I do not say that it was an approved institution. I shall show, on the contrary, that great efforts were made to suppress it, and they were partially successful. Yet it so fell in with the humour of the people that it constantly reappeared, and as under certain conditions it was innocent, it was tolerated for a time or in places. Church-ales, from the time of the year at which they were generally celebrated were often called *Easter-ales* or *Whitsun-ales;* and the place in which they were held was called the church-house.

Of church ales, Strutt says in his "Sports and Pastimes"[1]:—"The church-wardens, and other chief parish officers, observing the wakes to be more popular than any other holidays, rightly

[1] Book iv.

conceived, that by establishing other institutions similar to them, they might draw together a large company of people, and annually collect from them gratuitously, as it were, such sums of money for the support and repairs of the church as would be a great easement of the parish rates. By way of enticement to the populace, they brewed a certain portion of strong ale, to be ready on the day appointed for the festival, which they sold to them ; and most of the better sort, in addition to what they paid for their drink, contributed something towards the collection. But in some instances the inhabitants of one or more parishes were mulcted in a certain sum according to mutual agreement."

John Aubrey, writing in 1670, of Wiltshire, says :—" There were no rates for the poor in my grandfather's days, but for Kington St Michael (no small parish), the church-ale of Whitsuntide did the business. In every parish is, or was, a church-house to which belonged spits, crocks, &c.,—utensils for dressing provisions. Here the housekeepers met and were merry, and gave their charity. The young people were there too, and had dancing, bowling, shooting at butts, &c,, the ancients sitting gravely by and looking on : all things were civil and without scandal." [1]

[1] Quoted by Mr Carrington, in the Wiltshire Archæological Magazine, vol. ii.

It seems then that these ales served the purpose now sought to be obtained by bazaars and lotteries; though in truth this very English method of warming the heart for charity still survives literally in the custom of public dinners held annually by the patrons of charitable institutions. On rising to address such an assembly, a gentleman once began his speech in these very appropriate words: "Now, gentlemen, that we have eaten and drunk the cost of three orphans, we may proceed to the business which has brought us together."

Warton[1] quotes from a MSS. of a date previous to the Reformation, as is proved by the mention of an abbot, probably John Stanton, the last abbot of Dale, in Derbyshire:

"Memd., that this is the agreement betwixt the inhabitants of the townes and parish of Elvaston, Thurlaston, and Ambaston, of the one parte, and the inhabitants of the town of Okebrooke within the parish of the said Elvaston, on the other parte, by John, abbott of the Dale. . . . That is to say, that the said inhabitants of the said towne of Okebrooke shall brew fowre ales, and every ale of one quarter malt, and at theire owne costs and charges betwixt this and the feast of St John Baptist next cominge. And that every inhabitant of the said towne of Okebrooke shall

[1] History of Poetry, vol. iii. p. 119.

be at the said ales, and every husband and his wife shall pay 2d, and every cottyer 1d, and all the inhabitants of Elvaston, Thurlaston, and Ambaston, shall come to the said ales, and that every husband and his wife, and cottyer shall pay as is afore-rehearsed, and that the said inhabitants of Elvaston, Thurlaston, and Ambaston, shall have and reteine all the profits and vantages cominge of the said ales, to the use and behoofe of the said church of Elvaston. And that the said inhabitants of the said townes of Elvaston, Thurlaston, and Ambaston, shall brew viii. ales betwixt this and the said feast of St John Baptist, at the which ales and every each one of them, the said inhabitants of the towne of Okebrooke shall come to and pay every husband and his wife, and every cottyer, as it is above-rehearsed. And if hee bee away at one ale to pay at the toder ale for both, or els to send his money. And the inhabitants of the said towne of Okebrooke shall carry all manner of timber beinge in the Dale wood, new felled, that the said parishioners of the said townes of Elvaston, Thurlaston, and Ambaston, shall occupy to the use and profit of the said church."

Thus it appears that these ales had sometimes the character of hospitality given and received by neighbouring parishes on the occasion of their respective patron feasts.

## Drinking Customs. 115

Mr Carrington quotes also from the "Survey of Cornwall," printed in 1602, by Richard Carew, as follows :—

"For the church ale, two young men of the parish are yerely chosen by their last pregoers to be wardens, who, dividing the task, make collections among the parishioners of whatsoever provision it pleaseth them voluntarily to bestow. This they imploy in brewing, baking, and other achates against Whitsuntide, upon which holydayes the neighbours meet at the church-house, and there meetly feed on theire owne victuals, contributing some petty portion to the stock which by many smalls groweth to a meetly greatness, for there is entertained a kinde of emulation between the wardens, who by his graciousness in gathering, and good husbandry in expending, can best advance the churches profit. Besides, the neighbour parishes at those times lovingly visit one another, and this way frankly spend their money together. The afternoones are consumed in such exercises as olde and yonge folke (having leysure) doe accustomally weare out time withall.

"When the feast is ended the wardens yeeld in their account to the parishioners, and such money as exceedeth the disbursements is layd up in store to defray any extraordinary charges arising in the parish, or imposed on them for the good of the country, or the Prince's service, neither of which commonly gripe so much, but that somewhat still remayneth to cover the purses bottome."

The churchwardens' accounts of many parishes bear witness to the truth of this last statement. Thus in Kingston upon Thames, the proceeds of the church ale in 1526 are entered as £7, 15s., a sum that may be multiplied by twelve at least for its equivalent in modern money. In the churchwardens' books of Salisbury in 1469, a reference occurs to a collection made under the appellation of King's ale (Cerevisia regalis). The sum collected was £12, 16s. 6d. This was probably expended in the purchase of vestments, as there is an entry shortly after of £18, 3s. 4d. "for the new-fashioned vestments of crimson damask with eagles."[1]

It must not of course be understood that such large sums were realised by the mere sale of drink. The word "ale," in parish accounts, as well as "potation" in the constitution of guilds, or "propine" in old Scotch documents, corresponded to our word festival or dinner. It included the viands as well as the liquors; and as these were often supplied gratuitously by those who promoted the feast, and as a free collection was made in addition to the profits

[1] Sir R. Hoare's History of Wiltshire, p. 245.

## Drinking Customs.

from the entertainment, the custom must, as I have said, be considered similar to our charity bazaars and charity dinners.

I have in no way exhausted the list of methods for consuming drink known to our ancestors, but I have touched on most of those from which abuses might spring, and the knowledge of which is necessary to understand the church legislation, which I shall detail in a subsequent chapter.

## CHAPTER VII.

#### ACTION OF THE CIVIL POWER.

WE have seen that, for whatever reasons connected with race and climate, there has ever been a proneness in the inhabitants of these Northern Isles to the excessive use of intoxicating drinks. We have also seen what means of indulging this passion they had at their disposal, and what social customs arose from it or tended to encourage it. We have now to discover what measures, if any, were taken to suppress the abuses which arose, or to prevent them from arising. Drunkenness may be a social crime as well as a degrading and anti-Christian vice, and in modern times there has been much legislation with a view to diminish it. Hitherto the attempts have met with but little success.

The first thing then that must strike any one who reviews the history of civil legislation in England, on the subject of intoxicating drinks, is

## Action of the Civil Power. 119

that up to the period that is called the Reformation there is no civil legislation whatsoever against drunkenness. It is a crime not mentioned in the statute book until the fifth year of Edward VI. During that reign and subsequently many statutes were framed with the intention of punishing or preventing it. This fact, however, does not prove that the Reformation awakened a new zeal for morality in the nation; for drunkenness had not up to that period been unmolested or unpunished. A power had grappled with it, and that not unsuccessfully—the spiritual power of the Catholic Church ; and it was the destruction of this power in England and Scotland by the Reformation which, on the one hand, caused an immense and immediate increase of the vice; and, on the other hand, obliged the civil power to take upon itself a new office, which till then had been left to the Church, its natural ally.

In order to establish the truth of these assertions, it will be necessary to make a review of what was done in former times, by the civil power, as regards the subject of strong drinks.

We may begin our review with Scotland, since we have some curious information, going back to a very early period, in the history of that country. Mr Cosmo Innes, in his Preface to " Ancient Laws and Customs of the Burghs of

Scotland," tells us that the interesting code which stands at the head of that collection, is probably the oldest code of the kind now in existence. The customs of the principal burghs were gathered together and summarised in the reign of David I. (1124-1153), and are therefore, many of them at least, older than the twelfth century; while they became after that date the recognised law in all the burghs of Scotland for centuries.

From these, it appears that the brewing of ale and mead *for sale*, as well as the sale of wine, were at a very early period subjected to the control of authority. As duties were levied on the importation of wine, so also an excise was levied by the burgh on the brewing of ale, or to speak more accurately, a small sum was paid for a yearly licence to brew and sell ale—viz., fourpence yearly to the provost.[1] I do not see that any number was fixed of brewers to be licensed in a burgh. The publican sold the liquor he brewed himself; and it was forbidden to convey ale to another burgh for sale.[2] Outside a burgh no one could have a brew-house unless he had in the place furcam et fossam, "gallows and pit."[3] No one could sell ale unless it had been brewed for sale and previously tasted. The

[1] Leges Burgorum. 18.   [2] Ancient Laws, &c., p. 162.
[3] The gallows for hanging men, the pit for drowning women.

provost and other public officials of the burgh were altogether forbidden to brew ale or bake bread for sale; no doubt lest they should be bribed indirectly in the administration of justice, or lest they should draw customers by intimidation.

Public tasters were appointed who had to make oath to taste and lawfully apprise the ale, according to the price of malt, and in so doing to spare or favour no one.[1]

The measures in which the liquor was sold for consumption were to be all marked with the seal of the burgh.

The brewing and selling of the ale seems to have been an exclusively female occupation. One law runs as follows:—"What woman that will brew ale to sell shall brew all the year through, after the custom of the town. And if she does not, she shall be suspended of her office by the space of a year and a day. And she shall make good ale and approvable as the time asks. And if she makes evil ale, and does against the custom of the town, and be convicted of it, she shall give to her amercement eight shillings or be put on the cuck-stool, and the ale shall be given to the poor folk, the two parts, and the third-part sent to the brethren of the hospital. And right so doom shall be done of

[1] Ancient Laws, p. 129.

mead as of ale. And each brewer shall put her ale-wand outside her house at her window or above her door that it may be visible to all men. And if she do not she shall pay 4d fine."[1]

And to see that all these things were carried out, a public visitor of the burghs was appointed, called the Chamberlain. He had to inquire whether the brewster-wives took care to have their ale tasted and apprised, whether they sold it in pots of their own or in sealed measures, whether they refused to sell in the smaller measures, whether they filled up the measures to the brim with ale or only with froth, and how often they had been amerced in the year.

Regarding the tasters the visitors had to in-

[1] Leges Burgorum, p. 31. Philip de Harveng, Abbot of the Premonstratensian Monastery of Good Hope, in the diocese of Cambrai, gives incidentally a curious picture of the taverns of his time. (He died in 1189.) He is speaking of university students. Some, he says, care only for the insipid waters of Helicon, that is, for pagan writers, and despise the wine of Holy Scripture. These he compares to peasants, who never even ask the price of wine, but drink water from the nearest lake, or river, or cistern. Then he speaks of students who study Holy Scripture, not for their own profit, but merely to preach to others. He compares these to men who pass along the streets, and "as they pass by the taverns know, by the sign of the circle, that wine is sold there, and perhaps by the testimony of the crier know that it is good, yet they do not enter to taste it. Even if they are promoted to the office of crier themselves, and are eloquent on the strength and sweetness of the wine, what does it profit them if they never drink it?" Philip Ep. 3a. Migne Patrol, tom 203, p. 27.

quire whether they gave the brewers trouble, by not being ready at once to taste when the signal was given that the beer was to be put in the cask; whether they were bribed by drink; and to prevent this they were forbidden to taste inside the houses, but were to send in one of their number to choose which vessel should be tasted, and the experiment was to be made in the open street before the door of the house.

Similar precautions were taken in the gauging of wines and supervisions of the taverners.

In a constitution of William the Lion, it was ordered "That no baillie of our lord the King, nor any his servant, shall have a tavern in burgh, . . . on pain of the King's amercement unforgiven."[1]

Adulterators of wine were punished severely, and at a later period with cruelty, for an Act of 1482 decrees against these the penalty of death. Yet it is to be wished that our modern rulers would imitate their rude forefathers in protecting the people from adulteration, a very common cause of drunkenness; an assault on the health as well as a fraud on the purse of the public.

As regards England I find no civil regulations about liquor in any of the "Ancient Laws and Institutes" collected by Mr Thorpe, though local statutes like those of Scotland doubtless

[1] Ancient Laws, 203, p. 98.

were enforced in the towns. Towards the end of the twelfth century wines were more copiously imported than before; and in A.D. 1200, prices were fixed[1] for the different kinds of wines, both wholesale and retail. The retail price, however, was found to be impracticable, as it allowed no profit, and was immediately changed, and so, remarks the annalist, "the land was filled with drink and drinkers."

Henceforth the efforts of the civil power were directed to three ends; the encouragement of the wine trade with the Continental possessions of our kings; the supervision of it that both wholesale and retail dealers should use just measures, and sell unadulterated liquors at what were considered fair prices; and the raising of duties on the wine imported. As regards duty, the contrast is curious enough with our present rates. At first the king seized one tun before and one behind the mast.[2] In the time of Henry III., a duty of one penny on a tun was charged.

Even 400 years later, in the time of Charles II., the excise duties on a barrel of beer above 6d. the gallon was 1s. 3d.; and on a barrel of beer, under 6d. the gallon, only 3d.; on a hogs-

---

[1] See Burton Annals, at this date.
[2] Madox. History of the Exchequer, p. 526. This was called *Prisage*.

head of cider or perry, 1s. 3d.; on a gallon of mead one halfpenny; on a gallon of aqua vitæ one penny; on a gallon of coffee fourpence; and on a gallon of chocolate, sherbet, or tea eightpence. In 1670, brandy had a duty imposed on it of 8d. a gallon when imported, while the duty on coffee was reduced to 2d.

I need enter into no further details, on this head of customs and excise.

As regards the other ends aimed at by civil legislation, the attempts to guard against adulteration and to secure just measures were worthy of all praise. The attempts to fix the price seem to have been made in a blundering and vacillating fashion, whatever may be thought of them in principle. As they have only an indirect bearing on my subject, I will content myself with a bare record.

In 51st year of Henry III. (A.D. 1266), an Act was passed that when a quarter of wheat is sold for 3s. or 3s. 4d., and a quarter of barley for 1s. 8d., and a quarter of oats for 1s. 4d., then brewers in cities ought and may well afford to sell two gallons of beer or ale for a penny; and out of cities to sell three or four gallons for a penny. And when in a town three gallons are sold for a penny, out of a town they ought to, and may, sell four.

In another statute of the same year penalties

were enacted against brewers and venders who charged too much.

But if beer, being brewed everywhere, was sold cheaper in the country than in towns, where house-rent was higher, and grain had to be carried from a distance, the contrary was the case with wine, which was cheaper in the ports where it was landed than in inland towns.

Thus Edward I., in 1293 ordained, with the assent of the Gascon merchants selling wine in the city of London, that so long as a gallon of wine should be sold in that city for threepence, a gallon of wine should in Cambridge at all times of the year be sold for threepence-halfpenny only.[2] Mr Cooper, in his Annals of Cambridge,[3] mentions that thirty-seven years later, in 1330, the Chancellor and Masters presented a petition to Parliament, complaining that the above regulation was not carried out, and that high prices were charged for wine. He says that they obtained no redress. But in the statute-book, there is an Act of Parliament of that very year 1330 (4th Edward III.), as follows:—" Because there are more taverners in the realm than were wont to be, selling as well

---

[1] This and the following enactments are taken from the Statutes at large, unless where another reference is given.

[2] Cooper's Annals of Cambridge, vol. i. p. 66.

[3] Ibid., p. 85.

corrupt wines as wholesome, and have sold the gallon at such price as they themselves would, because there was no punishment ordained for them, as hath been for them that sell bread and ale, to the great hurt of the people," it was ordained that wine must be sold at reasonable prices, considering the port from which it was brought and expense of carriage; and that the wines should be tested twice a year—at Easter and Michaelmas—and oftener if needful, and corrupt wines poured out, and the vessels broken.

Several other statutes were passed in this reign regarding the prices of wine, which I need not enumerate. One expression in the preamble of the Act of 1365 is remarkable. "The King wills of his grace and sufferance that all merchant denizens, that be not artificers, shall pass into Gascoign to fetch wines thence, to the end and intent that by this general licence greater plenty may come, and greater market may be of wines within the realm; and that the Gascoigns and other aliens may come into the realm with their wines and freely sell them without any disturbance or impeachment." Yet such conflicting interests were at work, that four years later it was forbidden to Englishmen to fetch wines or even to buy them till landed; and this again was partly repealed the year after; and in 1378 (the 2d of Richard II.), aliens were allowed to sell wine in gross but not in retail.

The same vacillation appears in other respects. In 1365 an order of Council is issued for the seizure of all *sweet* wine, until further order.[1] In 1381 no sweet wines or claret could be sold retail, and the year following this prohibition was repealed. In 1387, it was enacted that no wine could be carried *out* of the realm. In 1483, the Lombard merchants bringing wine from the Mediterranean were obliged to bring bow-staves also for cross-bows; and in 1487, all wine from Guienne and Gascoign was to be imported in English ships—to keep up the English navy.

The last pieces of legislation of this sort which I need mention were in the reign of Henry VIII. By an Act of 1531, every beer and ale brewer was forbidden to take more than such prices and rates as should be thought sufficient, at the discretion of the justices of peace within every shire, or by the mayor and sheriffs in a city. By another Act of 1536, the price of French wines was fixed at 8d. the gallon, or 1d. the pint, under pains specified; that of Malmseys, Romneys, Sacks, and sweet wines generally at 12d. the gallon; and the Lord

[1] Rymer. Fœdera iii. 780.

## Action of the Civil Power.

Chancellor, Lord Treasurer, Lord President, and others, were to fix and proclaim the prices in gross.

We have thus passed in review the whole civil legislation previous to the Reformation. During this period the Church, as we shall see presently, was very busy in arresting the progress of drunkenness. The action of the State was confined to the procuring of a supply of good and wholesome liquor to be sold at moderate price.

In a subsequent chapter, we shall see how different became the spirit of the legislation when the influences of the Catholic Church were removed. But to understand this we must look for information, which the statute-book does not supply, as to the action of the Church. Our ecclesiastical documents are a field which English writers on temperance have not hitherto explored.

# CHAPTER VIII.

### ACTION OF THE CHURCH THROUGH THE SACRAMENT OF PENANCE.

THOUGH preaching comes naturally before penance, unfortunately I can give no adequate account of that great engine of the Church in England. There is perhaps no department of ancient English literature with which we have so little acquaintance as that of ordinary parochial sermons. The homilies of Venerable Bede were addressed to monks, as were those of St Ælred and of Adam Scot. The sermons that remain to us of John of Salisbury and of Peter of Blois were delivered to the clergy. The homilies of Œlfric, though intended for the people, were principally designed for festal occasions, as were most of the (lately published) "Blickling Homilies." The "Liber Festivalis," by John Myrc, as its name denotes, was intended to explain the feasts of the year rather than ordinary moral duties.

It was very much the practice in the Middle Ages for priests to preach to their flocks sermons which they had not themselves composed. Several zealous and saintly bishops made and published collections of such sermons for the use of the less instructed among their clergy. The homilies of Œlfric profess to be for the most part mere translations into Saxon-English of Latin discourses of St Augustin, St Jerome, St Bede, St Gregory, Haymo, and Smaragdus. Rabanus Maurus made a compilation of homilies for the use of the German clergy. St Cæsarius of Arles had done the same at the beginning of the sixth century, and his sermons had, even during his lifetime, been spread throughout Gaul, and were copied and preached over and over again for centuries, in the different countries of Europe.

I have given in the first part some specimens of exhortations on the subject of intemperance from St Cæsarius and from Rabanus. Whether the village pastors made use of these or similar collections, or whether they spoke from their own store; there can scarcely be a doubt that the people heard frequent admonitions regarding the national vice. In one of the "Blickling Homilies" it is said: "The bishop must lay a great injunction on the priests, if they will preserve themselves from the wrath of God, to tell

God's people, that on Sundays and Massdays they should diligently visit God's church, and joyfully hear there the divine instruction.

"The teacher shall not neglect the instruction, nor shall the people be too proud to humble themselves to him, if they desire God's forgiveness; for where the gospel is taught there many a man's heart is touched, and God will be merciful to the men who with meek heart believe in Him. Then must the bishop and the mass priests diligently urge men of all ranks and bid them rightly to observe God's decrees."[1]

The priest sows in the pulpit, but he reaps in the confessional. Perhaps at no time in England previous to the Reformation was confession what we should now call frequent. In the time of Venerable Bede the generality of Christians did not approach communion more than three times in the year; and at a later period once in the year was probably a much more common rule. Though this may seem very strange to us in the case of those who led pious and virtuous lives, and was indeed a subject of great regret to holy men like Venerable Bede; yet it need not surprise us in the case of those who fell sometimes into grievous sins. The severity of the penances then inflicted on sinners, while it must have effectually prevented many a relapse, must

[1] Dom. 3a in Quad., (Early Engl. Text Society, 1874).

also have no less effectually prevented such frequent confessions as are now so common. On the other hand, many a drunkard or other sinner, though Catholic in faith, now neglects altogether the sacrament of reconciliation, who in other days would have been compelled by human respect or the censures of the Church to make his confession, and by the exhortations of his confessor might have become a true penitent.

How then did the Church treat the drunkard when, by the exhortations of the preacher, the terrors of his own conscience, or the influences of the society in which he lived, he came to her in the character of a penitent? I have already said that the confessor was guided by rules which he was to study and apply with discretion to the special case before him. As I have passed in review the civil legislation on the subject of strong drink, so now I propose to review chronologically the legislation of the Church. Ecclesiastical documents on intemperance are frequent from the earliest times to the period of the Reformation in inverse proportion to the rarity of civil records. As we read them, though we may feel that we are studying a system of things quite different from anything with which we are now familiar, yet we shall find that they will throw light one on another, so that we shall understand enough to interest and instruct us.

## THE BRITISH CHURCH.

A.D. 569 synods were held by St David. Messrs Haddan & Stubbs give the canons[1] in what they believe to be their authentic form, from a transcript preserved in Brittany. On the subject of intemperance we have the following decrees. (Let me say, once for all, that in studying a matter so disgusting as drunkenness we must not shrink from crude forms of speech.)

1. "Priests about to minister in the temple of God and drinking wine or strong drink" (to excess) "through negligence and not ignorance, must do penance three days. If they have been warned, and despise, then forty days."

The ministering here referred to is not the celebration of the holy sacrifice. To offer that, after drinking even a draught of water, was a thing unheard of. The synod seems to speak of the divine office (*i.e.* the matins, vespers, and other hours), and the excess is supposed to be slight, not amounting to intoxication, yet sufficient to unfit them for joining becomingly in the psalmody. Many admonitions on the same subject occur in later cathedral legislation, and

[1] Ecclesiastical Documents, vol. i. p. 118.

they amount to saying that the clergy must study strict sobriety at their meals. The following canon, which speaks of real intoxication, imposes a much severer penalty :—

2. "Those who get drunk through ignorance must do penance fifteen days; if through negligence, forty days; if through contempt, three quarantains."

The nature of the penance is not here explained, as it was well known. It involved severe fasting, including abstinence from wine and beer. A quarantain, or forty days fast (in imitation of the fast of Lent), was a well-known term in the penitential system.

3. "He who forces another to get drunk out of hospitality must do penance, as if he had got drunk himself.

4. "But he who, out of hatred or wickedness, in order to disgrace or mock at others, forces them to get drunk, if he has not already sufficiently done penance, must do penance as a murderer of souls."

The above are the only relics of the ecclesiastical legislation of the British Church on our present subject which have come down to us, if we except the following canon, or rather monastic penance of St Gildas the Wise, in A.D. 570. "If any one (*i.e.*, a monk), through drinking too freely, gets thick of speech, so that he cannot join in the psalmody, he is to be deprived of his supper."

In order to appreciate properly the above and the following canons regarding monks, it should be remembered that the monastic system among the Celtic races in Britain and in Ireland, as well as among the Anglo-Saxons, took an immense development. A monastery was sometimes a village or town, with many hundred inmates. Most of these were laymen. They were recruited from all classes of society, and great criminals, no less than those who had been always pious and innocent, thronged into them. It would have been strange had they not brought with them some of their old bad habits.

Again, long fasting, united with hard manual labour, was their daily discipline. No wonder that when the refreshment hour came, the beer got into the heads of some.

Lastly, let it be remarked that the penitential canons provide for possible cases, and indicate nothing as to the frequency of a sin. In this they differ from the later legislation which was directed against existing abuses.

### THE IRISH CHURCH.

The present learned Bishop of Ossory, Dr

## Action of the Church. 137

Moran, remarks:[1] "To St Cummian Fota (an Irishman) was the Anglo-Saxon Church indebted for the penitential code which rendered it illustrious on the continent; and in the monasteries of Ireland were first drawn up those disciplinary canons which in a short time were adopted throughout the greater part of Western Europe."

Without wishing to deprive the Irish Church of any of its glory, I may remark that it must be shared with the British Church, with which it was in intimate communion. St David, St Gildas, and St Cadoc, British saints, visited Ireland between A.D. 544–565 to consult with the prelates of Ireland for the restoration of discipline in that country;[2] and the canons of St Cummian, who died in 662, are probably in great measure identical with those then drawn up. In any case it seems now generally admitted that "the great development of the penitential system in the West, which is usually attributed to St Theodore, had its beginning in the Celtic churches which he found in these islands."[3] The canons I am about to give, and which Dr Moran proves to have been drawn up by St

---

[1] Essays on the Origin, Doctrines, and Discipline of the Early Irish Church, by Dr Moran, p. 256. Dublin, Duffy.

[2] The proofs of this visit are given by Messrs Haddan & Stubbs, Ecclesiastical Documents, vol. i. p. 115.

[3] Ibid., Preface, p. x.

Cummian Fota, were frequently adopted by the churches, not only of England, but of Germany, France, Spain, and even Italy, from the eighth to the eleventh century.

Before quoting them it will be interesting to give an old legend concerning St Cummian:—
"Once upon a time that Guaire Aidhue, and Cumain Fota, and Caimine of Inis-Cealtra, were in the church of Inis-Cealtra, they were giving spiritual counsel to Guaire. 'Well, O'Guaire,' said Caimine, 'what wouldst thou have this church filled with?' Guaire answered, 'I would wish to have it full of gold and silver; and not from covetousness of this world, but that I might give it for my soul to saints and churches, and in like manner to every one that would ask for it.' 'But thou, O Cumain,' said Guaire, 'what wouldst thou wish to have in it?' 'I would wish,' said Cumain, 'to have it full of books to instruct studious men, and to disseminate the Word of God into the ears of all, to bring them from following Satan unto the Lord.' 'But thou, O Caimine, what wouldst thou wish to have in it?' Caimine answered them, and said, 'I would wish to have the full of it of disease and sickness to be on my body, and myself to be suffering my pain.' And so they obtained their wishes from God, viz., the earth to Guaire, wisdom to Cumain Fota, and sickness and dis-

ease to Caimine, so that not one bone of him remained united to the other on earth, but his flesh dissolved and his nerves, with the excess of every disease that fell upon him. So that they all went to heaven according to the wishes they had expressed in the church."[1]

Let us now listen to the wisdom of St Cummian. His Penitential has the following preface:[2]—"The difference of faults requires a difference of penances; for those also who cure the body compound diverse medicines for diverse kinds of ailments, and use various remedies according as they would cure wounds, or tumours, sores, bruises, or burns.... But as few only know this art of spiritual discernment, we will here indicate certain rules relating to the remedies of the soul, according to the traditions of our predecessors, and our own imperfect understanding in these matters; 'for we know in part, we prophesy in part' (1 Cor. xiii. 9). And before we tell how the remedies have to be applied to the wounds, according to the decrees of our fathers, we will give in a short abridgment a list of the remedies themselves. They are then as follows:—1. The remission which is received in baptism of water, according to the

[1] Translation of Dr Todd, Lib. Hymn., p. 87.
[2] The Penitential is published imperfectly in Bib. Max. Lug., tom. xii., and better by Wasserschleben.

words, 'Unless a man be born again of water and the Holy Ghost, he cannot enter into the kingdom of God.' 2. Charity, according to the saying, 'Many sins are forgiven her, because she loved much.' 3. Alms-deeds, 'As water quenches fire, so alms-giving quenches sin.' 4. Tears, 'Because he hath wept before me and walked sadly, I will not bring this evil in his days.' 5. The acknowledgment of one's crimes, 'I said, I will confess my sins against myself, and thou hast remitted the iniquity of my sin.' 6. Affliction of heart and body, 'I have judged . . . to deliver such an one to Satan for the destruction of the flesh, that the spirit may be saved in the day of our Lord Jesus Christ.' 7. Amendment of life, 'Thou art made whole; sin no more, lest a worse thing happen to thee.' 8. The intercession of the saints, 'Is any man sick . . . let him bring in the priests of the church; and let them pray over him . . . for the prayer of a just man availeth much' (James v. 14, 16). 9. Mercy, 'Blessed are the merciful, for they shall obtain mercy.' 10. The conversion and saving of others, 'He who causeth a sinner to be converted from the error of his way shall save his soul from death, and shall cover a multitude of sins' (James v. 20). 11. Indulgence to the faults of others, 'Forgive, and it shall be forgiven you.' 12. Martyrdom; our Lord, who is the only hope of salvation, having given it this privilege, and said to the penitent thief, ' To-day, thou shalt be with me in paradise.' "

It will be noticed that St Cummian does not place the sacrament of penance among these remedies, partly because he is treating explicitly of that sacrament, and partly because he considers it—which indeed is the true view—as the great means instituted by Jesus Christ of applying to souls other remedies, of exciting and exercising humility, contrition, love, mercy, alms-deeds, self-denial, and the rest.

It must be remembered that instructions similar to the above, stand at the head of the various penitentials. If we forget this we shall misunderstand all the following canons, which were not administered harshly and rigidly like prison discipline, but by a compassionate physician of souls, who encouraged his penitent to accept willingly whatever was hard to flesh and blood, and taught the spirit in which the penance should be performed, and the virtues by which it should be accompanied.

The judgments, then, of Cummian with regard to intemperance were as follow :—

1. "If a bishop or any one ordained has a habit of drunkenness, he must either resign or be deposed."

This is one of the apostolic canons.

2. "If a monk drink till he vomits, he must do thirty days' penance; if a priest or deacon, forty days. But if this happens from weakness of stomach, or from long abstinence, and he was not in the habit of excessive drinking or eating, or if he did it in excess of joy on Christmas or Easter Days, or the commemoration of some saint, and if then he did not take more than has been regulated by our predecessors (senioribus), it is not to be punished (nihil nocet).

"If the bishop urged him, the fault is not imputed to the monk, unless he gladly consented.[1]

3. "If a Christian layman vomit through drunkenness, let him do fifteen days' penance.

4. "If a priest gets drunk[2] through inadvertence, he must do penance seven days; if through carelessness, fifteen days; if through contempt, forty days; a deacon or monk, four weeks; a sub-deacon, three; a layman, one week.

5. "He who compels another to get drunk out of evil hospitality must do penance as if he himself had been drunk; if he did it out of hate he must be judged as a homicide."

Before proceeding further, one or two observations must be made. And first, that the penance was never imposed with mathematical

---

[1] Si Episcopus jusserit, non nocet illi, nisi ipse similiter.

[2] This must mean to a less gross degree than in the second canon.

rigour; that is to say, the penance to be imposed for a single act was not to be multiplied by the number of times the act had been committed, as in the penalties inflicted by human justice, though a much severer penance was inflicted on those who had been guilty of habitual sin than on those who had fallen only occasionally.

In the second place, it will be remarked that the penance inflicted on a layman was much less than that laid on a monk. In a still earlier penitential than St Cummian's, that of St Finnian, also an Irishman, for striking with the intention to murder, a half-year's penance on bread and water, followed by a year's abstinence from wine and flesh, was prescribed to a cleric, while to a layman for the same crime only one week's penance was assigned; and the reason given is that "for a man of the world guilt is less in this life, as the reward (of his mode of life) is also less in the next world." The disproportion in the case just mentioned will seem strange, unless we remember how much laymen in those days were exposed to the quick use of their weapons, whereas the clergy were forbidden even to wear them. In the case of drunkenness the disproportion was less.

It must not, however, be thought that all sins committed by "religious" are necessarily more grievous than similar sins committed by laymen. This will be the case with deliberate sins, and especially with public sins, because of scandal. But St Thomas[1] shows that an indeliberate sin, one of weakness or surprise, will have a less degree of guilt in proportion to the care that has been taken to avoid it; and that, therefore, should a monk sin, notwithstanding all the precautions he has adopted by his rule, provided the sin is not scandalous or deliberate, his sin will be less culpable before God, than the same sin committed by a secular who has been unwilling to surround himself with such restraints, and to use so many means of grace.

According to this doctrine, a fall into drunkenness by a man who has taken the pledge—if the pledge has not been intended for a vow, but only for an earnest resolution—will involve a less degree of guilt than an act of drunkenness committed by one who has refused to put himself under such restriction.

Reserving further explanation of the penitential system for a while, I will now detail the efforts which were made in England, after its second conversion by St Augustin and his companions and successors, to teach sobriety to Angles, Saxons, Jutes, and Danes, all (as we have seen) great drinkers by national tradition.

[1] S. Thomas, 2. 2ae. q. 186. art. 10.

## THE ANGLO-SAXON CHURCH.

St Theodore, a Greek, was sent to England by Pope Vitalian, and was Archbishop of Canterbury from 668 to 690. Several penitentials have been attributed to him, since his became the basis of many more. With regard to intemperance he merely repeats the judgments already given by the Celtic churches. The only addition to St Cummian is the following:—

"If a Christian layman drink till he vomits, he must do penance for fifteen days. But if he gets drunk, contrary to the prohibition of the Lord (in Lent?), if he have a vow of sanctity, he will do penance for seven days on bread and water, and then for seventy without flesh meat, but secular laymen without beer."[1]

St Willibrod (A.D. 692), the apostle of Frisia, has left some canons called Judicium Clementis (his other name). Among them occurs the following: "If a priest or clerk gets drunk himself, or makes another drunk; if he does this out of hospitality, he will do penance for forty days, but a layman for seven. If it is done through hatred, he will be judged as a murderer."[2]

There is much evidence that, at the end of

[1] Haddan and Stubbs, vol. iii. p. 177.
[2] Ibid., p. 226.

the seventh and in the beginning of the eighth century, when almost the whole of England was again nominally Christian, the half-converted English had brought into the Church some of their national vices, and that even the clergy, selected from this new race, did not always understand the sanctity of their vocation. Wihtred, King of Kent, at a Witenagemot held at Berghampstede, had to make the following regulation: "If a priest neglect the baptism of a sick person, or be drunk to that degree that he cannot perform it, let him abstain from his ministry until the doom of his bishop."[1]  A still more painful picture is drawn by Venerable Bede, in the letter he wrote to Egbert, archbishop of York, in 734, a little before his own death: "It is commonly reported of certain bishops," he writes, "that the way they serve Christ is this—they have no one near them of any religious spirit or continence, but only such as are given to laughter, jokes, amusing stories, feasting, and drunkenness, and the other snares of a sensual life—men who feed their belly with meats, rather than their souls with the heavenly sacrifice." About the same date St Boniface wrote from Germany to the Archbishop of Canterbury the admonition quoted in a former chapter. The extent of the evil and the

[1] Haddan and Stubbs, vol. iii. p. 234.

warnings of these holy men roused the vigilance of the pastors, and in a great council held at Clovesho by Cuthbert of Canterbury, and the bishops of his province, measures were taken to remedy abuses. The twenty-first canon relates to intemperance :—

"Monks and ecclesiastics," it says, " must not follow drunkenness, but shun it as deadly poison, since the apostle threatens that drunkards shall not possess the kingdom of God, and exhorts, 'Be not drunken with wine, wherein is luxury.' Nor let them force others to drink intemperately. Let their entertainments be pure and sober, not luxurious and accompanied by scurrility, lest their habit become contemptible among laymen, and deservedly infamous.

" If not compelled by infirmity, let them not drink before the canonical hour, *i.e.*, when tierce is finished (about ten o'clock), and not be the slaves of drink, like drunkards."[1]

The above canon is only an exhortation, but the general discipline of the Church provided the suitable penalties and remedies, and only needed to be enforced. We have two English

---

[1] Haddan and Stubbs, vol. iii. p. 369. It is scarcely necessary to remind the reader that beer was the ordinary drink at breakfast during the whole of the time we are reviewing. The clergy rose very early, and had been many hours fasting and singing psalms before ten o'clock.

penitentials of this period, one by Venerable Bede, the other by his friend Egbert, the archbishop. Bede, in his authentic penitential, merely repeats, on the subject of drunkenness, the judgments of St Cummian.[1] Egbert enters into more explanations. He first lays down the old canonical distinction, which had guided the legislation of the earliest councils, between capital crimes and lesser crimes. We must not confound this distinction with that between mortal and venial sins. The peccata minuta are often mortal sins,[2] and it is only in relation to canonical penance that they are thus measured. As regards intemperance, a *habit* of intoxication (ebrietas assidua) was a capital crime. This subjected those in holy orders to perpetual suspension. Occasional drunkenness, or the simple act (ebrietas as distinguished from ebriositas) is placed among the lesser sins.[3] For this, laymen are to do four or seven days' penance, clerks in minor orders seven or fourteen, subdeacons two or three

[1] See Haddan and Stubbs, vol. iii. p. 331. The Liber de Remediis Peccatorum is probably not Bede's, but a compilation from his penitential and that of Egbert.

[2] If any one doubts this let him read the 257th sermon in the Appendix to St Augustin (ed. Benedict).

[3] In one chapter the following definition or description of drunkenness occurs : "When the mind loses its usual state, the tongue stammers, the eyes do not see clearly, the head whirls, &c."

weeks, deacons three or four weeks, priests four or five weeks, and bishops five or six weeks.

But for all capital crimes, the penances were far more severe. Large alms were to be given and long fasting endured, according to the following proportion—a layman four years, a simple clerk five, a subdeacon six, a deacon seven, a priest ten, a bishop twelve. A priest who had been put to *public* penance could not be again admitted to the altar; at least this was rarely done before the ninth century.

Egbert repeats the canons of Cummian, just like St Theodore and St Bede.

The legislation of the Saxon Church was thus complete, and only required to be enforced. Unfortunately civil wars, and wars with the Welsh and the Danes, brought such confusion into the land, and gave rise to so much ignorance among the clergy, that discipline must have severely suffered. In the tenth century great efforts were made to restore discipline and learning, and amongst other matters drunkenness was not forgotten.

St Dunstan (A.D. 960), with King Edgar, drew up a code, in which the following canons occur [1]:—

Can. 26. "Let no drinking be allowed in the church."

[1] Wilkins' Concilia, tom. i. p. 225.

Can. 28. "In the festivals of the church all should be very sober and pray diligently, with neither drinking nor useless pastimes."

Can. 57. "Let priests beware of drunkenness, and be diligent in warning and correcting others in this matter."

Can. 58. "Let no priest be given to beer or buffoonery."

There is another collection of canons, put together by Œlfric (A.D. 970):—

Can. 29. "Let no priest drink immoderately, nor force others to do so, since he ought ever to be ready, if a child is to be baptized, or the Holy Eucharist given; and even if there is no such need, yet he should not be intoxicated, since God has forbidden drunkenness to his ministers."

Can. 30. "A priest should not drink in taverns like laymen."

Can. 35. "Do not exult over dead men, nor seek a corpse, unless any one accuses you. Then prohibit heathen songs and noisy laughter, and do not eat and drink where there is a corpse, lest you join in their heathendom."

On this subject of waking the dead, which resists the efforts of the pastors of the Church even to this day, we shall see many subsequent regulations. The 35th canon of Œlfric's collection is different in Spelman's edition, and is thus translated by Mr Thorpe [1]:—

[1] Laws and Institutes of England, vol. ii. p 356.

"Christian men should attend church frequently, and no one may discourse or conversation hold within God's church, because it is a prayer-house hallowed to God for ghostly discourses. Nor may one drink nor thoughtlessly eat within God's house, which to that is hallowed, that God's Body be with faith there eaten. Yet men now do too often foolishly, so that they will watch and madly drink within God's house, and play shamefully, and with idle speeches God's house defile. But for them 'twere better that they in their beds lay, than that they God angered in that ghostly house. Let him who will watch and honour God's saints, with stillness watch and make no noise. And let him who will drink and idly make noise, drink at his home, not in the Lord's house, that he God dishonour not to his own punishment."

I have shown in a former chapter how the customs here denounced had gradually crept in, and we shall have to return to this subject in viewing the ecclesiastical legislation of later times. But before we return to the work of the English Church after the Norman Conquest, it will be useful to study more minutely the old penitential system, and to see how the canons which we have passed in review were practically applied and with what results.

# CHAPTER IX.

### REMARKS ON THE PENITENTIAL SYSTEM.

IT may be useful, for the benefit of candid Protestants who have no personal experience of the Sacrament of Penance, and who would yet wish to judge correctly regarding so important an institution, and which has exerted so deep an influence for centuries upon millions of Christians, to make some remarks on the Penitential Codes we have been studying.

### PENANCE NOT UNSPIRITUAL.

First then, though I am not going to enter on the defence of the Sacrament of Penance, or to prove its divine origin, yet I think it necessary to guard against a fundamental misconception which might arise in uninstructed and still more in biassed minds in reading the rules which I have detailed in the preceding chapter. They might think that the whole system of pardon was an unspiritual, lifeless thing, a purchase of absolution at the cost of physical endurance of pain, according to a certain tax or tariff.

Some Protestant controversial books speak of the Sacrament of Penance as if it had little or no connection with all the various promises of forgiveness of sin contained in the Holy Scriptures, or their inspired lessons regarding the treatment of human passions—as if, even in the opinion of Catholics, it were intended not merely to supplement but to supplant such promises and such lessons. Nothing could be further from the truth. The institution of a sacrament of forgiveness did not make one promise void or one lesson superfluous. Our Divine Redeemer has purchased for us by His death, and instituted on the very day of His resurrection (see John xx. 19-23) a sacrament, in which all former promises to the penitent are being perpetually fulfilled, a channel for the conveyance of all Christian graces, and a school in which all lessons of virtue are continually taught, with a personal and practical force, such as they could never have when read in a book or listened to from the pulpit.

The popular error of controversialists in this matter is like that of the Jews, who, whenever they heard our blessed Lord say : " Thy sins are forgiven thee" (Luke v. 20, vii. 48), began to cavil at the words, instead of asking what disposition it was—what faith, and hope, and contrition, and love, and humility—which had won such gracious words for the happy penitents to whom they were spoken. Had they studied those dispositions in order to imitate them, they would not have merited our Lord's terrible reproach for not having done penance at the presence of His teaching and miracles (Matt. xi. 20), but would themselves have sought and obtained forgiveness and peace of heart. But their angry zeal for God's glory made them forget, not only their own souls, but all the circumstances in which our Lord's absolution was given. They only heard the formula of forgiveness, and of course heard even that amiss.

It would, I say, be an error akin to that of the Jews of old, if my Protestant reader, being startled at things to which he is unaccustomed, should fix all his attention on the mere external penance—the fast and the abstinence—and lose sight of the faith which accepted it, the contrition which accompanied it, the patience which supported it, the fear of God and self-restraint which grew out of it.

Nor is it only necessary to remember that the Church's penitents were human and immortal souls, redeemed by the Precious Blood, and moved by the Holy Ghost, and not animals fed or starved at the will of their masters; but it must also be borne in mind that the confessors or penitentiaries were also men, men with human sympathies, not task masters, aye, men who could often say with St Paul: "Who is weak and I am not weak? Who is scandalised and I am not on fire?" (II. Cor. xi. 29), and who knew how to yearn over their penitents, like a mother in labour, until Christ was formed in them (Gal. iv. 19).

At least let my reader observe that a penitential code gives by itself no more perfect a knowledge of the Sacrament of Penance than a catalogue of Materia Medica or Manual of Prescriptions gives of the healing art, of the learning and experience of the physician, of his quick judgment, or tender assiduity. A code is always a dry, lifeless thing; yet he is a dry and lifeless reader who is unable to give it life and animation by some knowledge of human nature, or some remembrances of history.

### PENANCE NOT COMPULSORY.

Now, to any one who reflects on the nature of the old penitential system, and the length of time during which it was in force, it must be clear that it exercised no slight influence in restricting the abuse of alcoholic drinks. For not only was intoxication severely punished, and punished too by penal abstinence from intoxicating liquors; but a similar abstinence formed part of the penance adjudged to every great crime. This abstinence was sometimes total for a period of years, sometimes it was intermittent, being enforced only on certain days in each week. Archbishop Egbert, in the introduction to his Penitential, in explaining the penance due to all capital crimes, such as heresy, murder, impurity, or perjury—a penance which, as we have seen, lasted for several years—remarks: "In each week the penitents abstain three days from wine, and mead, and flesh, and fast till evening and eat dry food; and their penance will be good if they remember the words of the Apostle: 'Whether ye eat or drink, do all to the glory of God.'"

No doubt, just as many committed crimes deserving of penance, so also many refused or neglected to undertake the penance due to the crimes they had committed. In other words, there were always weeds among the wheat in the Church's field, and bad fish in the Church's net, which refused to be changed into good fish. Still there were also multitudes of penitents, and who can doubt that such abstinence as has been described must have given birth to the spirit and power of self-restraint even after it was accomplished? For it must be carefully borne in mind that the instances in which the penance was compulsory (I do not say obligatory) were quite exceptional. In most cases it was the constraint of conscience alone that induced a man to accept his penance or to fulfil it. I do not, of course, mean that any age has been free from false penitents, or half-penitents, or from relapse. St Cæsarius, in a sermon addressed to public penitents,[1] warns them to persevere with the same fervour with which they have begun; and coming to the practice of fasting, says:—" If his health will permit it, let him take no wine; but if, on account of old age or weakness of stomach, he cannot altogether abstain, let him follow the Apostolic advice: 'Use a *little* wine on account of thy stomach.' There are penitents who are anxious to be soon reconciled, in order that they may be free to eat meat once more. But it is certain that he has performed his penance with too little compunction, who without necessity desires to eat meat. Even when he has been admitted to communion, he ought not" (during the period appointed for his penance) "to eat flesh-meat, if at his own or at others' tables he can have vegetables or small fish. I say this, because—what is still worse—there are penitents

[1] Sermo 261 in Append. S. Aug.

who eat meat greedily, and drink wine, and that even sometimes to excess."

A writer, probably of the twelfth century,[1] in answer to the question—"What do you say of public penitents?" replies, "Do not say penitents, but rather mockers of God. For they are such as 'rejoice when they have done evil and exult in iniquity.' When they have murdered they sing, when they have committed adultery they boast, when they have been guilty of perjury and sacrilege they joke. Though placed in penance they seek various kinds of drink, and strive to get drunk with many kinds of wine."

But this was written of men who were forced into external penance by ecclesiastical courts, and who were no more penitents than the inmates of modern jails and bridewells; and it was the scandal of such men being in any way connected, in the minds of the faithful, with the penitential discipline of the Church which caused the abolition of public penance, and the complete separation of the exterior from the interior court[2] or tribunal of conscience.

And just as the zeal and discretion of the

---

[1] Elucidarium, l. ii., n. 18, inter opera Honorii Augustodensis (Migne. Patrol, tom. 172). Also in the appendix to Gerberon's ed. of the Works of St Anselm. It is right to say that the author of this book is devoid of judgment, and exaggerates the vices of all classes of men.

[2] *Forum internum* and *forum externum*.

bishops modified the early canons, when, through the changes which had taken place in society, they ceased to be necessary or beneficial; so we may conclude that holy and learned prelates would not have sought, as they did, to enforce those canons for so many centuries, or have looked to their enforcement as the great means of reforming their flocks, had not their own observation convinced them that the penitential system exercised a powerful influence in favour of morality.

### PENANCE NOT UNIFORM.

I have said that the canons were not enforced with the rigidity of the penalties imposed by civil courts. Even when penance was imposed by the bishop or his official in the external court, the penitent was committed to the care of his immediate pastor, and the rigour of his penance was relaxed or maintained, shortened or prolonged, according to the dispositions which he manifested. But such public penance seems to have been almost unknown in England. St Theodore (A.D. 680) says:—" There is no public reconciliation in this province because there is no public penance;"[1] and the canons drawn up under King Edgar (A.D. 960), after describing

[1] Haddan and Stubbs, vol. iii. p. 187.

the mode of public penance, add—" These rites are observed beyond the sea."[1]

In the imposition of private penance a still greater discretion was allowed to the confessor. In fact the canons were like the rules for treatment of disease laid down in medical books, to be combined and modified according to the state of the patient. This comparison is made use of by St Dunstan in his treatise on penance, which begins as follows:—

### ST DUNSTAN ON PENANCE.

"In confession the help of a theologian is necessary, just as a good physician in the cure of a sick man.

"Rigorous penance is necessary to cure grievous sins, but always according to measure, and the canons of the Church. Inquiry must

---

[1] Wilkins, i. 231. Dr Lingard, in his History of the Anglo-Saxon Church, writes as if the contrary was the case. I do not know what were his authorities. It is true that an old English Homily, lately published by the Early English Text Society (anno 1873, Old Eng. Hom., p. 60), speaking of the beginning of Lent, says:—"So doth every bishop, who is in his minster, and driveth out the guilty men, who have to do those things which pertain to their shrift, and who shall do their penance until the Thursday before Easter-day, and then he will fetch them into the Church." But this was in the twelfth century, and perhaps the sermon itself was but a translation from the French.

## Remarks on the Penitential System. 161

also be made regarding the penitent's strength and his compunction. Some must do penance for a year, some for longer, some for a month or more, some only for a day, and some all the days of their life.

"If the physician will work a perfect cure he must use good medicines; but no wounds are so bad as those of sin, by which a man merits eternal death, unless by confession and abstinence and penance he be cured.

"Hence the physician must be wise and prudent who would heal such wounds. The beginning of the cure is good teaching; after that the poison must be got rid of by a good confession. Every one must cast up his sins by good teaching and confession, just as by a good emetic a deadly sickness is thrown off. The physician cannot cure any one till he gets rid of the poison, nor can he be taught true repentance who will not confess, nor can a man without confession correct his sins.

"After confession a man by penance can easily gain the mercy of God, if he lament in his heart that by the temptation of the devil he has been led into sin.

"The spiritual physician therefore must be prudent. He must know his penitent's necessary occupations in life, and take account of his

L

state and means of satisfaction, and grief and care for his salvation."

The Saint then goes on to explain in detail how the different classes of men, the magnates, the rich, the poor, and the sick, can do penance according to their state. But I have quoted enough for our present subject; and will only add a few remarks regarding commutation of penance.

### Commutation of Penance.

Besides such modifications as became necessary, from the varying circumstances of the penitents—such as ignorance, poverty, slavery, age, sickness, occupations—the confessor had to consider the disposition of his penitent and his grace of compunction. If the sinner had received from God a deep feeling of contrition, and was willing to punish himself to the utmost for his crimes, this might sometimes lead the confessor to impose upon him, for his good, the full amount of penance assigned by the canons; while, on the other hand, it might be a lawful cause of dealing more leniently with him, especially of shortening a penance once imposed and performed with fervour.

On the other hand, while an imperfect spirit of repentance would be in itself a reason for dealing with a soul more severely; yet the fear lest severity should drive into recklessness and despair, would cause the confessor to mitigate the just penance for such weak souls. He would remember, on the one hand, how our divine Lord "would not bruise the broken reed nor quench the smoking flax;" and on the other, how St Paul, after delivering the incestuous Corinthian to Satan for the destruction of the flesh, that the spirit might be saved in the day of our Lord Jesus Christ (1 Cor. v. 5), yet afterwards, on proof of his sincere repentance, wrote to the Church of Corinth "to pardon and comfort him, lest perhaps he should be swallowed up with overmuch sorrow" (2 Cor. ii. 7).

Such condescensions and mitigations required much spiritual discernment in him who made them, and we must not be surprised if they were sometimes granted from human respect and even from interested motives. Nothing can be more stern than the language in which the English bishops, assembled in the Council of Clovesho (A.D. 747), denounce the abuse which was then creeping in of commuting the penance of great men into endowments of monasteries: "Let not alms," say the fathers, "be given to lessen or commute satisfaction by fasting, and the other works of expiation, which have been canonically enjoined by God's priests for crimes, but rather for the penitent's greater amendment and the more speedy appeasing of God's indignation, which has been aroused by sin. Let the penitent know that the more he has been guilty of unlawful acts, the more he should abstain from what is permitted, and the more evil he has done, the more should he present to God fruits of good works, and not lose or lessen one good work by another. It is a good work to sing psalms; it is a good work to genuflect frequently with pure intention; it is good to give alms daily. But yet abstinence must not be given up on account of these, nor the fasts once appointed according to the Church's rule; without which no sins are remitted."[1]

On the other hand, such zealous reformers as St Boniface, St Willibrod, Egbert, and St Dunstan gave their sanction to various commutations of fasting into prayers, masses, and especially into alms-deeds and works of mercy. Thus St Dunstan draws a picture of a man devoting himself to a life of penance, laying aside his arms, making long pilgrimages barefoot, fasting and watching much, praying earnestly day and night, entering no warm bath nor soft couch, tasting no flesh meat *nor any intoxicating drink*, and the rest; adding that "he is no doubt cruel to himself who condemns himself to such a life

[1] Haddan and Stubbs, vol. iii. p. 373.

as this, yet he is blessed if he cares for nothing but to correct his sins." The saint then continues: "But there are various forms of penance, and many men may redeem their sins by almsdeeds. If a man has riches he may build a church for the glory of God, and if able endow it with land, and induce ten young men to serve it; or he may repair churches, mend roads, build bridges over deep streams or miry roads; he may give large alms to widows, orphans, and strangers, manumit his slaves, or purchase slaves to manumit them, especially those taken in war; give food, clothing, roof, hearth, bath, bed to the poor; get masses said and psalms sung, and chastise himself by severe abstinence from food and drink and every luxury of the body."

I will pause here to make a suggestion to those who are accustomed to speak slightingly of the ways of their Catholic forefathers. A great part of the expenses of government is paid at the present day by revenue raised on liquor. This may be necessary, but it is certainly not honourable to England. On the other hand, England owes no little of her present freedom and civilisation to the penances imposed by the Catholic Church in former days on her penitent children. The roads on which we drive, the bridges which span our rivers were, in many cases, first made at the suggestion of a

Saxon priest to his rich penitent. The churches in which many an Anglican clergyman preaches against Popery were first built in humble atonement for drunkenness, violence, or impurity; and the lands from which the same gentleman and his family now draw their revenue were dedicated to the priesthood and the poor of the Catholic Church by means of the sacrament of penance. And still more, the free working classes of England, and many even of the middle and higher classes, are the descendants of those slaves and serfs who were emancipated, at the instance of the Church, by those rich landowners, who shrank, perhaps, from the severity of penitential fasts, and embraced the easier form of penance which men like St Dunstan suggested as a substitute. No one, I think, who has looked into the history of slavery in England will be inclined to contest the truth of this assertion.

There would be more wisdom and more humility in the country if some of those who talk so loudly of liberty, and who speak of confession as a degradation to a free-born Englishman, would reflect that perhaps they owe it to the sacrament of penance that they are freeborn; and might, if they would, from the same sacrament acquire that far higher liberty "wherewith Christ has made us free" (Gal. iv. 31)—freedom from the tyranny of their passions.

## CHAPTER X.

ACTION OF THE CHURCH IN HER SYNODS.

THE severity of the ancient penitential system was gradually relaxed, and by the thirteenth century had attained its present mitigated form. It is needless to discuss how far this mitigation has been a loss to souls. It was rendered necessary, not only by decay of faith and prevalent corruption of morals, but by the altered circumstances of society. In rude times the State had gladly left the punishment of many criminals to the Church, and had been satisfied when they accomplished the penance imposed on them by the canons. But when the State took on itself the administration of justice, and that too with no slight severity, the Church could not punish over again, with the old rigour, those who had already suffered so much for their crimes. It is true that offences like that of mere drunkenness did not fall under the cognisance of civil tribunals; but it was of course found impossible to maintain the canonical penalties for lesser offences when those for greater crimes had been relaxed.

Thus Alexander Stavenby, bishop of Coventry, in the instructions on the sacrament of penance which he published in 1237, writes that "since penances are now arbitrary, we do not define for confessors any fixed penance which they must impose."[1] He merely requires that they shall be medicinal and appropriate and proportioned to the vice.

But if the rigour of sacramental penance was relaxed in the Middle Ages, the zeal of the bishops against sin did not decline; and as the Church, as well as the nation, became more united, and the clergy less rude, synods were more frequent for the preservation of discipline.

In the present chapter we shall see how much the vice of intemperance has occupied the attention of the prelates of the Church in England, and by what means they have sought to combat the various abuses to which the national propensity to excessive drinking gave birth.

St Anselm had been urged by the Pope to labour at the reformation of clergy and laity, and had received ample spiritual powers for the purpose. In 1102 he proclaimed the following

[1] Wilkins' Concilia, tom. i. p. 646.

canon in the Provincial Council of London:
" That priests should not go to drinking assemblies nor drink down to the pegs " (ad pinnas).[1]

It would seem from this that the measure taken by St Dunstan to correct deep drinking,[2] had been perverted by the ingenious malice of men into a new provocation to intemperance. As the frequenters of taverns were forbidden to drink below the pegs fixed in the bowls, they seem to have challenged each other to drink at least down to the pegs, presumably in one draught.

I do not find any new legislation during the succeeding century; but the habits of conviviality had so spread throughout Europe as to call for the action of a General Council.

The fourth of Lateran (A.D. 1215) decreed as follows:—" Let all the clergy carefully abstain from gluttony and drunkenness. Let them be moderate in the use of wine,[3] nor let any one be urged to drink, since drunkenness, while it suspends the powers of the soul, excites the lusts of the body. We therefore decree that the abuse must be utterly abolished, which prevails in certain places, that drinkers bind themselves to drink as much as their fellows; so that, in

---
[1] Wilkins' Concilia, tom. i. p. 382.
[2] See pp. 78 and 105.
[3] Vinum sibi temperent et se vino.

their judgment, he receives most praise who intoxicates a greater number, and himself drinks deeper draughts. If then any (cleric) commit these sins, unless after being warned by his superior he gives thorough satisfaction, let him be suspended from his benefice or office." [1]

This Council gave a great impulse to the legislation of national, provincial, and diocesan synods, and we trace its influence in England throughout the thirteenth century.

Even two years before the General Council of Lateran in A.D. 1213, an assembly of the king, bishops, and nobles of the realm had been held at St Alban's,[2] in which it was proclaimed to the viscounts, foresters, and other ministers of the king, as they loved their life and limbs, not to make any violent extortions, nor dare to injure any one, or to hold *scot-ales* anywhere in the kingdom as they had been wont to do." This prohibition was renewed two years later in the famous charter granted at Runymede, and in the Charta Forestæ, A.D. 1225, and frequently confirmed.

I have explained in a previous chapter the nature of a scot-ale (or ale shot, as it was sometimes called). That which was forbidden by

---

[1] Colet. Concil. tom. xiii. p. 951. The canon was drawn up both in Latin and Greek.
[2] See Matthew Paris. Hist. Maj. p. 239, ed. Wats.

these charters was a mode of extorting money. It will be remembered that royal "forests," or uncultivated lands, formed at that time no small part of England, and that they were not subject to the common law. The king's officers took advantage of this immunity to exercise great tyranny over the people, and previous to this period sought to raise money by setting up taverns and drinking assemblies, which the country people were compelled to frequent for fear of incurring the displeasure of their petty tyrants. Modes of raising money, different in form, though similar in their nature and consequences, are by no means unknown to publicans at the present day; and labouring men, in order to get hired, have sometimes to purchase the good-will of the master of the beer or gin shop in which workmen assemble and wages are paid. It will be a happy day when a new Magna Charta shall rescue the nation from the tyranny of the "liquor interest," whether it be that of the great brewers and distillers, or of the petty-vendors.

But scot-ales, as I have said, though abused by the foresters, were not confined to the forest-lands. The evil, indeed, had grown to such a height, that from one end of England to the other a great effort was made by the bishops to suppress them. I give these decrees in their chronological order. They will require little commentary.

A.D. 1220, Richard de Marisco, Bishop of Durham, published[1] the decree of the Council of Lateran given above, and then added "We forbid announcements of scot-ales to be made by a priest or any one else in the church; and if priest or cleric do this, or take part in a scot-ale, he will be punished canonically."

A.D. 1223, Richard Poore, Bishop of Sarum, decrees: "We order that no announcement of scot-ales be made by laymen in the church, and neither in the churches nor out of the churches by priests or by clergymen."[2]

A.D. 1225, a National Council was held in Scotland, in obedience to Pope Honorius III., to carry out the Lateran decrees. The sixty-second chapter warns the clergy to beware of drunkenness, and entirely to avoid taverns, except in case of necessity, on a journey.[3]

A.D. 1230, the famous Robert Grossteste, Bishop of Lincoln, in the instructions issued to his archdeacons, orders inquiries to be made: "Whether 'rams' are erected any-

---

[1] Wilkins' Concilia, tom. i. p. 574.
[2] Ibid., p. 600.
[3] Ibid., p. 616; see also the decrees in the Register of the Church of Aberdeen, published by the Spalding Club.

where to get up a scot-ale."[1] Six years later he wrote a very interesting letter to his archdeacons on various abuses to be eradicated. He mentions especially the vice of drunkenness, and its causes and consequences:—"Because no one can succeed," he says, "in subduing other vices, who has not controlled gluttony and drunkenness, we first of all strictly command that you prohibit in your synods and chapters those drinking assemblies which are commonly called scot-ales; and every year, in every church of your archdeaconries, this prohibition must be several times made known; and if any presume to violate this prohibition canonically made, you must admonish them canonically, and proceed against them by ecclesiastical censures."

The archdeacons are also to watch over the wakes or vigils of the saints'-days, that they be not the occasion of scurrilities: and also to take care that at funerals, the house of mourning, where the last end of man should be remembered as a remedy against sin, be not changed into a house of laughter and jokes for the multiplication of sin.[2]

A.D. 1236, St Edmund, in his Constitutions, repeats those of the bishop of Durham, publish-

[1] Wilkins, i. 628.
[2] Grossteste Epist. 22 and 52 (Rolls ed.)

ing the decree of Lateran, and denouncing scot-ales.[1]

A.D. 1237, Alexander Stavenby, Bishop of Coventry, forbids, "under penalty of half a mark, any priest to go to a tavern, or to keep a tavern or scot-ale. The same bishop published[2] a very interesting instruction on the seven capital vices, and on the administration of the sacrament of penance.

About the same date, some statutes which have been preserved, though it is not known to what diocese they belonged, "forbid priests or clerics to frequent taverns, or to dare to keep them in their own houses or in other houses. They forbid also any announcement of scot-ales from being made in the church by the priest or by clerks outside."[3]

I may be allowed to remind those who are not acquainted with Catholic discipline, that the word "clergy" does not necessarily mean priests. A clerk or cleric was any one who had received the clerical tonsure. There were in the whole period preceding the Reformation great numbers of clerks in England in minor-orders, or simply tonsured, besides deacons and sub-deacons. Many of the former class were married, but they were subject to ecclesiastical rules.

[1] Wilkins, tom. i. p. 635.   [2] Ibid., pp. 640-646.
[3] Ibid., p. 662.

In A.D. 1240, Walter of Cantilupe, Bishop of Worcester, published the following constitution:—[1] "We forbid the clergy to take part in those drinking parties, called scot-ales, or to keep taverns. They must also deter their flocks from them, forbidding by God's authority and ours, the aforesaid scot-ales, and other meetings for drinking."

A.D. 1255, Walter de Kirkham, Bishop of Durham, wrote:—"We adjure all priests, by Him who lives for ever, and all the ministers of the Church, especially those in holy orders, that they be not drunkards, nor keep taverns, lest they die an eternal death, according to the threat of the law—Vinum et omne quod inebriare potest non bibetis tu et filii tui, ne moriamini" (Lev. x. 9).

"Moreover, we forbid Scot-ales and games in sacred places, as it was done by the constitution of our fathers and predecessors." [2]

A.D. 1256, Giles of Bridport, Bishop of Salisbury, decreed:[3]—"By this synodal approbation we confirm the prohibition of scot-ales, which has been made for the good both of souls and bodies; and in virtue of obedience we command rectors, vicars, and other parochial priests, that by frequent exhortations they earnestly

[1] Wilkins, p. 672     [2] Ibid., pp. 705, 707.
[3] Ibid., p. 719.

induce their parishioners not rashly to violate this prohibition. Should any do so, let them be denounced as interdicted from entering the church or receiving the sacraments, until they go to our penitentiary, whereupon their penalties will cease, but they will receive from him such penance for their transgression as he may enjoin, and with the help of God fulfil it.

"By common potations we mean when more than ten of the same parish, in which the beer is sold, or even of the neighbouring parishes, come together for the sake of drinking in these taverns, or in the ground surrounding them; but we do not comprise in this prohibition strangers who are travelling and those who come together in fairs and markets, although they meet in taverns."

In A.D. 1257, Walter, Bishop of Norwich, issues similar instructions to those of other bishops, against the clergy keeping or frequenting taverns.[1]

In A.D. 1287, a Synod of Exeter does the same.[2]

The abuse of scot-ales seems to have yielded before these repeated assaults of so many bishops, for we hear little about them in later times.

In A.D. 1342, however, a council held in London

[1] Wilkins, p. 732.  [2] Ibid., tom. ii. p. 144.

## Action of the Church in her Synods. 177

had once more to abolish wakes over the dead on account of drinking and buffooneries;[1] and in A.D. 1350, William Russell, Bishop of Sodor, had again[2] to warn the clergy of his remote diocese against taverns and drinking assemblies under pain of three months' suspension.

In A.D. 1364, a synod of Ely adopts almost the very words of Bishop Grossteste (given above) about excess of drink among the clergy, and scot-ales.[3]

In A.D. 1367, John Thoresby, Archbishop of York, complains that in vigils, men come together in the churches and at funerals, as if to pray, and then turning to a reprobate sense, they indulge in games, and vanities, and even worse, by which they greatly offend God and the saints, whom they pretend to venerate; and they make the house of mourning at funerals a house of laughter and excess, to the great ruin of their souls. Wherefore all rectors and vicars are commanded to put a stop to these abuses, and will be fined twenty shillings (to be applied to the fabric of the cathedral) if they neglect to do so; while those men who have rendered themselves guilty of such offences are to be *ipso facto* interdicted from entering the churches which they have profaned,

[1] Wilkins, tom. ii. p. 706.　　[2] Ibid., tom. iii. p. 11.
[3] Ibid., tom. iii. p. 60.

M

and cannot hear the divine offices, or receive sacraments till they have made satisfaction."[1]

I have mentioned the custom of distributing at funerals and at anniversaries doles of bread, ale, and meat, otherwise called give-ales. Warton mentions,[2] that in 1468, the prior of Canterbury and the commissaries made a visitation (the See being then vacant), and it was promulgated that potations made in the churches, vulgarly called give-ales or bride-ales, should not further be in use, under the penalty of excommunication.

As an appendix to this chapter, I may add an example or two of "Sunday closing" which, however, belong neither to the legislation of the Church nor to that of the State, but to that local legislation which many would wish to see revived. In A.D. 1428, the corporation of Hull made an order for the observance of the Sunday; no market was to be kept, under penalty of 6s. 8d. for sellers, and 3s. 4d. for buyers—no butchers were to expose meat for sale, nor cooks to dress or sell except to strangers, and to them only before eleven o'clock; no tradesmen to keep shops open; no vintners nor ale-house keepers to deliver or sell ale under the same penalties.[3]

[1] Wilkins, iii. p. 68.  [2] History of Poetry, vol. iii. p. 119.
[3] Hadley's History of Hull, p. 59.

A similar attempt may be found recorded in the Burgh Register of Aberdeen,[1] about the same date.

It is probable that if the records of our old cities were searched, similar regulations might be found. London made an attempt to suppress Sunday-trading, but it was ineffectual.

" In the year 1444," says Fabyan, " was an Act made by authority of the Common Council of London, that upon the Sunday should no manner of thing, within the franchise of the city, be bought or sold, neither victual nor other thing; nor none artificer should bring his ware to any man to be worn or occupied that day, as tailor's garments or cordwainer's shoes; and so likewise of all other occupations; the which ordinance," adds Fabyan, " held but a while."[2]

The rarity of the documents which have come down to us does not permit me to illustrate my subject from the history of Ireland in the later Middle Ages. Indeed it is uncertain, as I have already said, whether, until comparatively modern times, there was any general abuse of alcoholic liquors, which would call for further action on the part of the prelates of the Church, than such as belongs to all pastoral vigilance,

---

[1] Published by the Spalding Club.
[2] Chronicle of England, p. 617 (ed. Ellis).

the instructions of the pulpit and the purifying and repressive influences of the confessional.

The following decrees do not belong to the time I have undertaken to illustrate, yet they will serve to show how carefully the zeal of the Irish prelates has guarded the sobriety of the people.

A Provincial Synod held in Kilkenny, in 1614, by the Archbishop of Dublin, Dr Eugene Matthews, enacted many excellent statutes which were "the chief code of ecclesiastical discipline and law for more than two centuries to the Church of Dublin."[1]

In the chapter regarding the holiness of life befitting priests, they are forbidden to enter taverns for drinking, unless they should be on a journey, or to take part in drinking assemblies; even though they should not themselves drink to excess.[2] There is, however, nothing to show that any special abuse had called for this statute, which is merely precautionary, and such as may be found enacted by similar synods of the Church in every age and country.

But a Provincial Synod of Armagh, held in 1618, gives an account of some abuses which

---

[1] Dr Moran, Lives of the Archbishops of Dublin, p. 266. These statutes have been printed in full in his Appendix, pp. 439-463.
[2] Ibid., p. 455.

had sprung up, and which it endeavours to extirpate. Among these were "excessive luxury in funeral banquets," both among the rich and the less wealthy, leading to buffooneries and indecencies even in the presence of the dead body; also the celebration of baptismal and nuptial festivals with excess; and the patron feasts whether of churches or of religious orders, to provide for which the laity were burdened "to supply cows, sheep, calves, lambs, goats, deer, birds, and a variety of wines and other liquors," to the great grief and scandal of the good, &c. These customs were all prohibited, and the statutes of this synod were adopted by the other provinces of the Island.[1] In 1632 a Provincial Synod was held in Galway by the Archbishop of Tuam, Malachy O'Quigley, who died a martyr at Sligo in 1645.[2] Among the regulations which concern the clergy we find the common one against drinking in taverns, except in case of necessity; while they are exhorted to remove the causes of intemperance from themselves and from others, by putting a stop to challenges or provocations to drink (*æquales haustus*).

---

[1] Dr Moran. Ibid., p. 273. See the statutes given at length in his Appendix, pp. 427-431.

[2] Given in the additional notes to Dr Moran's Life of Archbishop Plunket, pp. 384-389.

Another Provincial Synod of Armagh, held at Clones in 1670, forbids priests and the clergy in general to frequent taverns or markets, under pain of privation of benefice after a third admonition.[1]

In the Provincial Synod of 1678, held at Ardpatrick, we have special mention of spirits: "We decree that no priest drink distilled waters (*aquam stillatam*) in any tavern, or public meeting, under pain of a fine of ten shillings."[2]

Both these synods were presided over by the famous Oliver Plunket. Few prelates have been more zealous against intemperance than this holy martyr. And in no words could this long series of records be better closed than in those which he wrote to the Sacred Congregation of Propaganda:—

"Whilst visiting six dioceses of this province I applied myself especially to root out the cursed vice of drunkenness, which is the parent and the nurse of all scandals and contentions. I commanded also, under penalty of privation of benefice, that no priest should frequent public-houses, or drink whisky, &c.

"Indeed I have derived great fruit from this order, and, as it is of little use to teach without

---

[1] Given in the additional notes to Dr Moran's Life of Archbishop Plunket, p. 128.
[2] Ibid., p. 134.

## Action of the Church in her Synods. 183

practising, I myself never drink at meals. Give me an Irish priest without this vice and he is assuredly a saint."[1]

[1] Given in the additional notes to Dr Moran's Life of Archbishop Plunket, p. 78.

## CHAPTER XI.

### RESULTS OF THE WITHDRAWAL OF THE CHURCH'S INFLUENCE.

IT is admitted on all hands that the change of religion in the sixteenth century was accompanied by a great outburst of immorality; but the apologists of that change have said that this was but a passing effect of the unsettlement of men's minds, and that the permanent result of Protestant doctrines and influences was beneficial. The evidence of the national statute book is altogether opposed to this theory, as I shall now show, by taking up the review of civil legislation from the reign of Edward VI., where we broke off in a previous chapter.

The spirit of this legislation is entirely different from that which had preceded the Reformation. There is, indeed, the same or rather a far greater desire to raise revenue by means of the liquor traffic, and attempts are still made to regulate the prices; but, besides this, complaints are made of the spread of drunkenness, sumptuary laws are passed, licences required for ale-houses and taverns, and at last, penalties inflicted on the drunkard.

In 1552 (5th Edward VI.), "forasmuch," says the statute, "as intolerable hurts and troubles to the commonwealth do daily grow and increase through such abuses and disorders as are had and used in common ale-houses and other houses called tippling houses," it is enacted that justices can abolish ale-houses, and that none can be opened without licence.

The above statute merely regarded the sale of beer, but two years later, "for the avoiding of many inconveniences, much evil rule and common resort of mis-ruled persons used and frequented in many taverns, *of late newly set up in very great numbers* in back lanes, corners, and suspicious places within the City of London, *and in divers other towns and villages within this realm,*" it was enacted that licences should be required to sell *wine*, and that not more than two taverns could be licensed in a borough, with the following exceptions:—Forty in London, and three in Westminster, eight in York, six in Bristol, four in Norwich, Hull, Exeter, Gloucester, Chester, Canterbury, Cambridge, and Newcastle; three in Lincoln, Shrewsbury, Salisbury, Hereford,

Worcester, Southampton, Ipswich, Winchester, Colchester, and Oxford. A price was fixed for the wines, and no wine could be sold to be drunk on the premises.

"And be it further enacted that it shall not be lawful to any person, except he shall dispend in lands, tenements, hereditaments, or other yearly profits certain, the sum of 100 marks, or else he be worth of his own proper goods and chattels 1000 marks, or shall be the son of a duke, marquis, earl, viscount, or baron of the realm—to have or keep in his house or custody any piece or vessel of any of the wines of Gascoign, Guyen, French, or Rochel wines, containing above the quantity of ten gallons, to the intent to spend or drink the same in his house by any colour or means." I do not see that any penalty was decreed for the violators of this prohibition or any means appointed to discover them; and from the account given by Holinshed of the state of things under Elizabeth, it is clear it must have remained a dead letter. We have seen acknowledgment by the legislature of the recent increase of drinking among the poor; that luxury kept pace with it among the rich will scarcely be doubted after reading the following passage :—

"As all estates do exceed herein, I mean for strangeness and the number of costly dishes, so these forget not to use the like excess in wine, insomuch as there is no kind to be had neither anywhere more store of all sorts, than in England (although we have none growing with us, but yearly to the proportion of twenty or thirty thousand tun and upwards brought over to us), whereof at great meetings there is not some store to be had. Neither do I mean this of small wines only, as claret, white, red, French, &c., which amount to fifty-six sorts, but also of the thirty kinds of Italian, Grecian, Spanish, Canarian, whereof Vernage, Cate piment, Raspis, Muscadell, Romnie, Bastard, Tire, Oseie, Caprike, Clareie, and Malmeseie are not least of all accounted of, because of their strength and valure."[1]

Testimonies might be multiplied to the increase of drunkenness during this reign. Cecil complained that "England spendeth more in wines in one year than it did in ancient times in four years."[2] In 1597, an Act was passed "to restrain the excessive use of malt." In the preamble, it is asserted that "greater quantity of malt is daily made than either in times past, or now is needful." Justices were empowered in quarter sessions to suppress the making of malt and the number of maltsters.

[1] Holinshed's Chronicles, i. 167.
[2] Quoted by Mr Green in his History of the English People, p. 388.

The author of the chapter on Manners and Customs in Knight's "Pictorial History"[1] says: —"Excess in the use of wine and intoxicating liquors was now the common charge against the English: and it seems to be borne out, not only by the quantity consumed, but by the extent to which taverns had multiplied by the end of Elizabeth's reign."

The same writer gives curious details of the drinks then in fashion. Besides "fifty-six different kinds of French wines, and thirty-six other kinds, of which the strongest were most in request, distilled liquors were now frequently made in England, the chief of which were rosa solis and aqua vitæ. This last spirit became very plentiful, in consequence of great numbers of Irish who settled in Pembrokeshire in the reign of Henry VIII., and devoted themselves to the distillation of their national beverage, which, as it was both good and cheap, had an extensive sale over the kingdom."

As to beer and ale, there was single beer or small ale and double beer, and double-double beer, and dagger-ale and bracket. "But the favourite drink, as well as the chief article of vulgar debauch, was a kind of ale commonly called huffcap, but which was also called maddog, angel's food, dragon's milk, and other such

[1] Vol. ii. p. 884.

ridiculous names, by the frequenters of ale-houses; and never, says Harrison, did Romulus and Remus suck their she-wolf with such eager and sharp devotion as these men hale at huffcap, till they be as red as cocks and little wiser than their combs. The higher classes, who were able to afford such a luxury, brewed a generous liquor for their own consumption, which they did not bring to table till it was two years old. This was called March ale, from the month in which it was brewed. A cup of choice ale was often as richly compounded with dainties as the finest wines. Sometimes it was warmed, and qualified with sugar and spices; sometimes with a toast, often with a roasted crab or apple, making the beverage still known under the name of Lamb's-wool; while to stir the whole composition with a sprig of rosemary was supposed to give it additional flavour. The drinks made from fruit were chiefly cider, perry, and mum. Those that had formerly been made from honey seem to have fallen into disuse, in consequence of the general taste for stronger potations; metheglin being now chiefly confined to the Welsh."

But if habits of drinking to excess prevailed in the reign of Elizabeth, they certainly suffered no decrease under James I.

The statute of 1604 runs thus :—" Whereas the

ancient, true, and principal use of inns, alehouses, and victualling-houses was for the receipt, relief, and lodging of wayfaring people travelling from place to place, and for the supply of the wants of such people as are not able by greater quantities to make their provision of victuals; and not meant for entertainment and harbouring of lewd and idle people, to spend and consume their money and their time in lewd and drunken manner;—it is enacted that only travellers and travellers' friends, and labourers for one hour at dinner-time, or lodgers, can receive entertainment," under penalty of fines specified.

This Act seems to have been still-born, for only two years later (in 1606) another Act was made " for the better repressing of alehouses, whereof the multitudes and abuses have been and are found intolerable, and *still do and are likely to increase.*" This only provides that beer is not to be sold by merchants, to men who have no licence to sell.

But in the same year 1606, an attempt was made to punish the buyers as well as the sellers. "Whereas," says the statute, "the loathsome and odious sin of drunkenness *is of late grown into common use* within this realm, being the root and foundation of many other enormous sins, as bloodshed, stabbing, murder, swearing, fornication, adultery, and such like, to the great

## Withdrawal of Church's Influence. 191

dishonour of God and of our nation," &c., therefore a fine of five shillings was imposed for drunkenness, and three shillings for tippling in alehouses, except as allowed by the Act of 1604; and for second offence the offender was to be bound over to good behaviour.

We must praise the perseverance of these legislators, if we cannot applaud their success; for three years later (in 1609), they try once more. " Whereas," they say, " notwithstanding all former laws and provisions already made, the inordinate and extreme vice of excessive drinking and drunkenness *doth more and more abound*," &c.—they enact that offenders convicted against the last two acts shall be deprived of their licence.

The legislature in this reign seems to have been more active than the executive, for in 1623 (21st James I.), the last statute has to be renewed just as if it had ceased to be in force.[1] In 1621 there were no less than thirteen thousand public-houses licensed in England.[2]

In 1627 (3rd Charles I.), a fine of twenty

---

[1] No wonder. James was known to be an habitual drunkard. Ladies of high rank copied the royal manners, and rolled intoxicated in open court at the king's feet.—*Green's History of the English People*, p. 473.

[2] Rev. Mr Raines, in a note at p. 12 of Chetham Miscellanies, vol. v. (1875).

shillings, or whipping, is imposed for keeping alehouse without licence.

Perhaps this last enactment gives the explanation of an entry in the churchwardens' accounts of the parish of Mortlake-on-Thames, in 1646—" for a frame and a whip that hangs in the church for drunkards, 1s."

I need pursue the subject no further, for my object is not to review the efforts of modern civil legislation, but to illustrate the efficacy of the ancient ecclesiastical influences in England. For this purpose it was necessary to show that, whatever work the Church did, she did single-handed. She did not call the State to her aid, at least by any statutes of the realm; though she willingly accepted the co-operation of local magistrates, which does not seem to have gone beyond an occasional closing of taverns on Sundays. But with the exception of such slight assistance, the Church alone coped with drunkenness in England for more than a thousand years.

Was she successful? Or did she succeed to such an extent as to make it worth while for the friends of temperance to study her methods?

These were the questions I had proposed to myself to solve. But it is not easy to estimate success in a negative work, or one of repression. The question arises as to what would have been the state of England in regard to this vice independently of the Church's action. If the answer was not to be a mere conjecture, it was necessary to ascertain what was the intemperance before her influence was exerted, and what it became when that influence was removed. That the Angles, the Saxons, the Danes, were mighty drunkards in their heathen state and continental homes, we know. The Church had, therefore, a difficult work to do. We know also that her efforts were only partially successful, for drunkenness to some extent continued to characterise the Christian inhabitants of England. But that she laboured zealously has been proved by abundant evidence, and that she laboured not without success is already made evident by the rapid and continued increase of drunkenness as soon as her influence was withdrawn. For what is there to account for the change which followed the Reformation, but the absence of the old repressive powers of the Church? There was no great increase of population, no sudden affluence, no new relations with the Continent making the importation of liquor cheaper. Yet our statute-book bears witness that drunkenness made a sudden and alarming progress from the very beginning of the Reformation, and that in spite of every effort of the Legislature it continued to spread throughout the realm.

Queen Elizabeth put aside the Catholic priesthood and the Sacrament of Penance in 1559. Exactly one hundred years later, in 1659, the following character of England was sketched by a French Protestant [1] :—

"There is within this city (London), and in all the towns of England which I have passed through, so prodigious a number of houses where they sell a certain drink called ale, that I think a good half of the inhabitants may be denominated alehouse keepers. These are a meaner sort of *cabarets*. But what is more deplorable, there the gentlemen sit and spend much of their time, drinking of a muddy kind of beverage and tobacco, which has universally besotted the nation, and at which, I hear, they have consumed many noble estates.

"As for other taverns, London is composed of them, where they drink Spanish wines, and other sophisticated liquors, to that fury and intemperance, as has often amazed me to consider it. But thus some mean fellow, the drawer, arrives to an estate, some of them having built fair houses, and purchased those gentlemen out of their possessions, who have ruined themselves

---

[1] See the pamphlet in the tenth volume of the Harleian Miscellany, p. 193, seq.

by that base and dishonourable vice of ebriety. And that nothing may be wanting to the height of luxury and impiety of this abomination, they have translated the organs out of their churches to set them up in taverns; chanting their dithyrambics and bestial bacchanalias to the tune of those instruments, which were wont to assist them in the celebration of God's praises, and regulate the voices of the worst singers in the world, which are the English in their churches at present. . . .

"A great error undoubtedly in those who sit at the helm, to permit this scandal; to suffer so many of these taverns and occasions of intemperance, such leeches and vipers, to gratify so sordid and base a sort of people with the spoils of honest and well-natured men. Your lordship will not believe me, that the ladies of greatest quality suffer themselves to be treated in one of these taverns, where a courtezan in other cities would scarcely vouchsafe to be entertained. But you will be more astonished when I shall assure you that they drink their crowned cups roundly, strain healths through their smocks, dance after the fiddle, kiss freely, and term it an honourable treat. . . .

"Drinking is the afternoon's diversion; whether for want of a better, to employ the time, or affection to the drink, I know not. But I have found some persons of quality, whom one could not safely visit after dinner, without resolving to undergo this drink-ordeal. It is esteemed a piece of wit to make a man drunk, for which some swilling insipid client or congiary, is a frequent and constant adjutant."

Such was the state of England a century after the destruction of the Catholic Church, in spite of all the progress that commerce, science, and literature had made. Assuredly no such picture could have been drawn of Catholic England in the worst of times. I do not mean, by what I have said, to attribute the increase of drunkenness to the positive and explicit doctrines of the new religion. Human reason condemns drunkenness as well as revelation. Plenty of denunciations of the vice might be gathered from Protestant sermons preached during the century that followed the Reformation. Acts of Parliment condemn it as "a loathsome and odious vice," and "the root and foundation of many more." But it is also true that doctrines were preached which, indirectly and contrary to the intention of the preachers, loosened the bonds of morality. And, still more, the sacrament of penance had been removed, without which preaching loses more than half its power; and the belief in the Presence of Jesus Christ in the holy Eucharist had been taken away, a belief which had been the main impulse to the frequentation of the Sacrament of Penance and the purifying of the conscience.

The nature of the present work, which is not controversial, prevents me from dwelling more on this subject. I trust, however, that enough has been said to convince even the prejudiced that the Holy Spirit of God has ever moved the Catholic Church to fight against the works of the flesh, and has crowned her efforts with no insignificant victory in the past ages. Enough, too, has been said to prove to Catholics that they need not look outside the Church for methods of combating vice. The very difficulties with which we have now to contend have arisen in no slight measure from the abandonment of those arms of offence and defence which the Spirit of sanctity forged for His Church militant on earth. At the same time, we must remember that it would be vain and futile to regard with complacency the victories of our fathers unless we imitate their prowess. A terrible battle is before us. The sons and daughters of the Catholic Church are being slain by thousands by this abominable vice of intemperance. While, then, we take courage from the past, let us also learn wisdom. I will endeavour in the concluding chapter to gather together some of the principal lessons taught us by the preceding history.

## CHAPTER XII.

### CONCLUSIONS AND SUGGESTIONS.

I HAVE already stated that the present work was not undertaken in order to advocate, and much less in order to oppose, any modern method of attacking the vice of intemperance in drink, which may be either sanctioned or tolerated in the Catholic Church. I am not indifferent to questions of total abstinence or partial abstinence; of pledges and temperance societies, of Sunday closing or permissive legislation. But I have endeavoured to pursue an historical investigation unbiassed by such topics, though not without the hope that some practical aid might be thus secured towards the solution of our present difficulties—that we might become more fixed in our principles by the wisdom or authoritative teaching of those "who have spoken to us the word of God" (Heb. xiii. 7), and that we might learn prudent and vigorous action from their successes or even from their failures.

The following observations, therefore, in no way aim at a complete statement of principles, but are merely intended to fix the reader's attention to certain conclusions which seem to flow from the preceding history, and to prevent any hasty generalisation being made, without attention to time and circumstances, from any authorities I have quoted, or facts which I have mentioned.

## THE CIVIL POWER.

First, then, although I have repeatedly remarked that the Church before the Reformation received little or no help from the civil government, I most certainly do not wish to imply that no aid should be sought at the present day. It is often said that legislation cannot make men sober. But to this it has been truly answered that bad legislation can make men drunk, by multiplying temptations.

The Apostle ordered prayers to be made "for kings, and for all that are in high station, that we may lead a quiet and peaceable life in all piety and chastity" (1 Tim. ii. 1, 2). The early Christians had no control over their legislators and rulers, and could only pray that God would direct them. In our present society, without neglecting prayer, we may use all lawful human efforts to obtain the same ends. In the word "chastity" is most certainly included, directly or indirectly, sobriety; and bad legislation is one of its most dangerous enemies.[1]

The review which we have concluded has shown how wars and civil commotions, and bad or imperfect government, may hamper, paralyse, or overbear the beneficent action of religion. Nothing really grand and lasting will have been done to meet *national* drunkenness until its causes have been thoroughly investigated and extirpated, so far at least as good laws can extirpate them. But these causes are very many; some lie in our inherited physical propensities, some in our climate, some in our occupations, some in our amusements, and some in our literature. A thousand agencies are required, a thousand reforms must be made, before the nation can become sober. My object is not to discuss these various reforms, but merely to see what the Catholic Church can do, what true religious

---

[1] On this subject I refer my readers to Dr Lees' Prize Essay, called an Argument for the Legislative Prohibition of the Liquor Traffic, published by the United Kingdom Alliance, Manchester; or by Tweedie, 337 Strand, London (price 1s. 6d.), which I advise all to procure. It is full of information which will be useful even to those who cannot admit all its conclusions.

principles and legitimate methods we must embrace, in order at least partially to correct an evil, over many of the causes of which we have little control. In the meantime I would guard myself against being supposed to maintain that religious influences need no assistance, or that religion does not cry out for the removal of the causes and temptations of drunkenness. Most certainly, though the Catholic Church is militant, she has no wish to multiply the difficulties of her warfare; and she will ever welcome whatever good measures may be taken by the civil legislature to promote the health of the people, the cleanliness and comfort of their dwellings, their necessary recreation, their moral and intellectual elevation; or, on the other hand, to prevent the noxious adulteration of liquor or the multiplication of allurements to the weak.

### SNARES TO FAITH.

But if Catholics may stand on the same platform with any of their fellow-subjects in agitating for good civil legislation, they will never co-operate with those who would promote temperance from mistaken principles of morals, or by a system of morality divorced from religion. And Catholic pastors will ever watch that none of their flock get inveigled into those associations in which errors are taught regarding the use of God's creatures, or in which temperance is converted into a fantastic form of Deism. For this reason the Holy See condemned the "Sons of Temperance" in America, and Catholic bishops in England and Ireland have warned their flocks against the "Good Templars." The members of such associations deny, indeed, that they oppose the Catholic faith, and profess to leave every man free in matters of opinion, while they unite them on a broader platform of morality. There are, of course, many unions amongst men, having a moral aspect, from which all questions of faith may be excluded; but temperance societies are hardly of the number. Temperance is no doubt a natural virtue, and has its own natural motives and sanctions. Abstractedly it is possible (though by no means desirable) to confine attention to these. But in reality this is seldom done. On the contrary, the advocates of abstinence in the associations of which I am speaking, have ever been accustomed to exalt abstinence both in its moral and religious aspects. Yet while doing so they profess "to interfere with no man's religion." They call on their hearers "to sink their religious differences," and to associate on another basis. The tendency of such exhortations and associations has been, and always will be, to treat dogmas and sacraments as superfluous, and to exalt temperance into a form of natural religion. Why should Catholics, who are certain of their faith, and whose faith is to them a bond of union and not a cause of division, forego these advantages and expose themselves to error or exaggeration, while in a purely Catholic association temperance may hold its proper place, though it will be enforced by more urgent motives, and practised by more powerful aids?[1]

Some will call these principles narrow and sectarian, and will term it liberal and Catholic to make common cause with all enemies of drunkenness. But as the Infinity of God does not consist in His comprising all things in Himself, as Pantheists dream, but rather in His exclusion of all things finite, so the Catholicity of the Church is in herself and her own sufficiency for all souls, and not in her union with human sects and tolerance of human errors.

### Need of Grace.

Again, the teaching and the action of the

---

[1] See the letter of Dr Kenrick, Bishop of Philadelphia, to Cardinal Franzoni, and the Rescript of the Congregation of the Holy Office, condemning the Sons of Temperance (20th August 1850), among documents of the Plenary Council of Baltimore.

Church in past ages impress on us the necessity of closely associating all efforts to promote temperance or to repress intemperance with the helps supplied by religion.

I feel it unnecessary to discuss what are the powers of unassisted human nature in the matter of abstinence. I am writing for Catholics in the British Isles, in America, Australia, or elsewhere, exposed by their national customs to intemperance, and living in the midst of temptations. I may presume that very few of such can hope to persevere long in the practice of temperance, without having to encounter danger more or less serious. In past times it might have been an exaggeration to say this of women, at least in the higher classes. It is to be feared that even among them the danger is becoming less remote.

But even could we assure ourselves of perseverance in sobriety without the use of the appointed channels of grace, we should require God's help to make our abstinence fruitful to salvation.

There are also snares in the path of the total abstainers as well as of the moderate, which can with difficulty be avoided without the help of religion.

It is admitted by all theologians that a great temptation cannot be *conquered* without the help of grace; but, on the other hand, they remark that an apparent though delusive victory may be gained by many stratagems of nature. Thus one vice may often yield place to another. Drunkenness may make room for spiritual intoxication; and a man's mind may be so turned to religious fanaticism that the temptations of his former gross vices yield to the greater seductions of his new and more dangerous vices of the soul. That pride and fanaticism too often overcome the reformed drunkard is a trite remark. The old Catholic penitential system was a powerful remedy against this danger. It thoroughly associated sin with shame and humiliation. It would never tolerate such a spectacle as may have been sometimes witnessed even in our Catholic temperance halls, of a once notorious drunkard humorously relating his experiences to an applauding audience.

I would not be understood to say that we must use no agencies which are not distinctly spiritual, or that we can co-operate in no work which is not raised on a distinct foundation of faith. We may surely use natural methods to make a drunkard a man, before we attempt to raise the man into a Christian. I would only say that no methods which do not lead to the means of grace should be regarded as final or as free from danger.

## THE PLEDGE.

What has been said of the need of grace applies especially to the observance of what we now commonly call the pledge.

The principle of renouncing the use of fermented drinks for the sake of edification, or for greater security, was approved by Origen, even when combating false principles of abstinence. Some Catholics in his day in the zeal of their hatred of heresy were opposing indiscriminately all who refused intoxicating drink. Origen warned them that they were indiscreet, and might be doing mischief.[1] St Bernard, too, while denouncing the heretical abstinence taught by the sects, was careful to add, "If they were guided by spiritual physicians and ascetic discipline, I should approve of their virtue."[2]

Let not, then, anything I have said in this book be misunderstood, as if it were intended to oppose the zealous endeavours of modern reformers, on the ground that they have no precise precedent in Catholic antiquity. I should fear, were such my intention, to incur the reproach which God made of old to some of the Jews:— "I raised up of your sons for prophets, and of your young men for Nazarites; and you will

---

[1] See in chap. i. p. 4.   [2] Ibid., p. 9, 10.

present wine to the Nazarites, and command the prophets, saying, Prophesy not" (Amos ii. 11, 12).

He would indeed show ignorance of the spirit of Christian antiquity who should oppose anything excellent merely because it is modern. When the military orders sprung up in the twelfth century for the delivery of the Holy Land, it was no doubt a novelty; but was it on that account esteemed uncatholic? Far from it. St Bernard praised God for the new grace. "A new kind of warfare," he writes, "is now heard of in the earth, new and unknown to former ages. Soldiers there have always been, monks have abounded. But when we see both the exterior and the interior man each girt with his own belt and bearing his own sword, who is not filled with admiration at so great and so novel a prodigy? Rejoice, then, O Jerusalem, and know the time of thy visitation. Rejoice and praise, O thou who wast deserted, for the Lord has consoled His people, and prepared for us a holy and a mighty arm in the sight of the nations."[1]

The captivity of Christian souls in the bonds of intemperance is a sadder evil than that of the Holy Land under the yoke of the Saracens, and if God has raised up brave men for their de-

[1] S. Bernardi Exhort. ad Milites Templi.

liverance, it would ill become us to complain that the mode of their warfare is new. Our only anxiety must be that the new weapon be used with ancient valour, and that the new soldiers fight under the ancient standards.

 I am distinctly of opinion that the evil of intemperance is now so deep-rooted and widespread, and its occasions so frequent, that precautions are now generally required, which in other days may have been superfluous. Again, owing to the use of ardent spirits, cases which in old theologians might have been discussed as extraordinary and almost monstrous, have become of frequent occurrence; and remedies which were extreme may now be usual and almost necessary. For these, then, and other reasons which I need not mention, the pledge, though little known to history or to theology, has grown into a legitimate and most beneficial discipline.

 It is from this conviction that I am the more anxious to save it from the disrepute into which it has been at times brought by the ignorance or indiscretion of some who have taken it. It is a most useful auxiliary when guarded from abuse; and I believe that I am but echoing the warnings of many zealous promoters of the pledge, when I mention some of the dangers to which it is exposed.

## Conclusions and Suggestions. 209

It must then be taken with a correct knowledge of its purpose and its obligation, and made a help and not a substitute for religion. The pledge may be taken from different motives: as a practice of Christian mortification—as a means of edifying and influencing others—as a precaution against danger. But it is well known that some who keep it for a limited period, at the expiration of the time they have fixed, and sometimes even on the very day on which their pledge expires, rush headlong into drunkenness. They do not seem to have understood that the purpose of their temporary abstinence ought to have been to protect them until they had broken through evil habits, shaken off bad associates, and learned, in the practice of their religion, a habit of self-command. St Cæsarius said of some Christians of his own day, who observed the Church's fast rigidly until sunset, and then gave way to excess in eating and drinking at the evening meal, that "they dined late but did not fast." Would it be too severe to say of some who give themselves to drunkenness, after they have observed their two years' pledge, that they have endured privation rather than practised abstinence?

The pledge is also sometimes taken as if, by the supposed holiness of him who gives it, it would work a sudden physical or moral change, and relieve him who takes it from his unnatural craving or make him victorious without a combat. St Augustin warned his hearers not to expect such an effect from baptism. It cannot therefore but be useful to dispel such delusions with regard to what is not a sacrament, and has no sacramental grace unless taken in the Sacrament of Penance. These are the words of the holy Doctor:[1]—" Let us suppose," he says, " that a man who has been a drunkard is baptized. He has heard with fear drunkenness enumerated among the crimes which exclude from the kingdom of God (1 Cor. vi. 9, 10). He has trembled at these words. He has been baptized, and all his sins of drunkenness have been forgiven him. But there remains the bad habit. Though he is regenerate he has an enemy to fight against. All his past vices are forgiven; but he must watch and struggle lest he should chance to get drunk. The desire of drink rises up and tickles (titillat) his soul, and his mouth grows dry, and his senses are tempted. The lust would, if it could, break through the wall, enter the enclosure (of his soul), and make him captive. Such is the attack. Repel it! 'Oh, that I had not this desire!' But if it grew from bad habit, by good habit it will die out. Only do not satisfy it, do not gratify it by yielding, but kill it by

[1] Sermo 151.

resisting. As long as it exists you have an enemy. If you do not consent to it, and never get drunk, it will become less and less every day. Its strength consists in your subjection. If you yield to it, and get drunk, you give it strength. You cannot say, 'I never heard about this sin.' You cannot say, 'God will require my soul at the hand of the priest, for he did not warn me.' You groan, for by bad habit you have made yourself a powerful adversary. It cost you no effort to make him powerful, but you must undergo much toil in conquering him; if you find yourself too weak ask help from God."

These last words of the saint are all important in this matter. It seems clear that if the ignorant—and who are more likely to be ignorant than habitual drunkards?—if such are to be prevented from seeking to turn the pledge into a charm, they must receive clear and detailed instruction on the nature and purpose of a pledge, as well as on the nature of the obligation incurred.

I am not speaking of the first warnings or exhortations by which the drunkard is arrested on his way to ruin, but of the instruction to be given to him before he makes his final resolution. St Aelred, an English Cistercian abbot of the twelfth century, writes:[1]—

[1] Speculum Charitatis, l. iii. cap. 34.

"There is an abstinence not imposed but voluntary, of which the Psalmist says: 'Voluntarie sacrificabo tibi.' It is a free holocaust, when a man gradually rises, from the enjoyment of what is lawful to the accomplishment of what is commanded, and so to the undertaking of such things as are only proposed to those who are ambitious of the more ample prizes of heavenly love. . . . Thus the forsaking of the world, the resolution of perfect chastity, or *the profession of any kind of special rigour of life*, are numbered among voluntary sacrifices. . . . Before undertaking what is sublime and perfect, let the aspirant diligently consider the exact nature of the vow or the resolution he sets before him; and then let him weigh well in the balance of experience his strength both interior and exterior—his interior strength to fight against daily temptations, and his exterior strength to sustain with unwearied patience the burden of bodily toil."

St Aelred here is not writing specially on abstinence from intoxicating drink; and it may, perhaps, be said that such abstinence involves no "special rigour of life," or that the "daily temptations" to drink, of those who abstain altogether, are much more easily conquered than the daily temptations to drunkenness of many who do not thus abstain. I do not deny, for my part, that this is often the case, and that a prudent spiritual physician may sometimes advise total abstinence as the safer and easier course.

The principle, however, laid down by the saint is very important. Even in renouncing sin men must act prudently and count the cost. This is the lesson taught us by our Lord when He speaks of the man that began to build the tower and was not able to finish, adding : "So likewise, every one of you that doth not renounce all that he possesseth, cannot be my disciple" (Luke xiv.) Self-denial is to the Christian what bricks and mortar are to the builder; and as a man should not begin to build without "reckoning the charges that are necessary" (Luke xiv. 28), so a soul should not offer itself to God without knowing what is involved in its offer. A man who takes the pledge should know clearly what he is promising or resolving to do, and what grace he must seek in order to keep his resolution. Too many, from neglect of this prudence, have exposed themselves to the mockery of their neighbours, saying, "This man began to build, and was not able to finish" (Luke xiv. 30).

For the same reason of prudence the extent of the obligation should be clearly ascertained.

St Anastasius of Sinai, a great authority in matters of asceticism, who wrote in the second half of the sixth century, asks [1]—"If any one make a good resolution, *such as to abstain from wine for a time*, or from flesh-meat, and afterwards, out of neglect, do not keep his resolution, what is to be done?" He replies—"First, he ought to condemn his own weakness and misery. Next, in the Euchologium,[2] there is a prayer for this end, by which the priest releases a man from an obligation; for priests have received from God power to bind and loose on earth and in heaven.... Wherefore," he concludes, "it is to be recommended not to bind one's self either to what is good or what is bad, for where there is obligation there comes transgression, as happened to Adam."[3]

### ASSOCIATION.

The evils of intemperance are so gigantic at the present day that they require all our united efforts to meet them. The principle of association is also pre-eminently Christian, and has special promises made to it by our Divine Redeemer. If, then, I make any remarks on our temperance associations, it is with a view to strengthen and not to weaken them.

[1] Bib. Max., tom. ix. p. 1036.    [2] The Greek Ritual.
[3] The "Pledge," as now authorised in the Catholic Church, is not a vow or oath, but a solemn resolution, or at most, a promise made to man.

## Conclusions and Suggestions. 215

The movement against drunkenness has been compared to the crusades, and I welcome it as St Bernard welcomed the outburst of Christian chivalry in his day. But, if I mistake not, one of the lessons of history is that the crusades of the Middle Ages greatly suffered when they were guided by popular enthusiasm, and especially when they were allowed to gather together an indiscriminated mass. Greater prudence in organising might have produced happier results.

We are not perhaps as yet thoroughly agreed as to all the measures which prudence will prescribe. We are still learners. In the meantime the variety of suggestions which have been made, is rather an advantage than a hindrance to the cause. The wants of one parish may not be those of another; nor are the powers, the opportunities, or even the views of those to whom the direction of the movement belongs, always alike. It is therefore useful to have a choice of methods; and I have gathered in an appendix the rules of several associations which have the approbation of our ecclesiastical superiors.

There is, however, one danger to which we are exposed by the variety of our confraternities—that of jealousy or mutual depreciation. Even religious orders have not been free from this bane to charity. Nothing is more admirable than the language with which St Bernard appeased the envy and detraction which were beginning to separate the servants of God in his time; and if we substitute Total Abstainers and Partial Abstainers in the place of Cistercians and Cluniacs, we shall find a most important and practical lesson in his words:—"What security, what quiet shall we find in the Church," he asks, "if every man when he has chosen one state of life, despises those who live differently, or thinks himself despised by them? When Christ ascended to his Father He left to His Spouse, the holy Church, His 'seamless tunic, woven from the top throughout' (John xix. 23). But the tunic, though seamless because of the charity which binds it in indissoluble unity, is many-coloured, because of the diversity of graces and of gifts. . . . What then? I am a Cistercian. Do I therefore condemn the Cluniacs? By no means. I love them, I extol them. Why then, you will say, do you not embrace the order which you praise? I answer with the Apostle: 'Let every man abide in the same calling in which he was called' (1 Cor. vii. 20). But you will ask again, why I did not choose it in the beginning, since I knew it to be good? I reply with the same Apostle:— 'All things are lawful for me, but all things are not expedient' (1 Cor. x. 22). The order indeed is holy, but I am carnal, and I knew the sickness of my soul to be such that a stronger medicine was necessary for me. Different remedies befit different diseases. You may often safely recommend to another what you abstain from yourself. . . . I praise then every order in the Church in which men live justly and piously. I belong to one by my mode of life, but to all by my charity. Oh! how great is the confidence of charity. One man toils without love, and another loves without sharing in the toil. The first toils in vain, but the second does not love in vain, for he makes the toils of the first his own. . . On the other hand, by rash judgment, and detraction, we lose the benefit of all our labours. 'I give thee, thanks, O God,' said the Pharisee, 'that I am not as the rest of men, extortioners, unjust, adulterers' (Luke xviii. 11). Why does He not add detractors? Is detraction so small an evil? No, for the Apostle says: 'Railers shall not possess the kingdom of God'" (1 Cor. vii. 10).[1]

These warnings of St Bernard were rather made as a precaution than on account of any existing evil, and for the same reason I have transcribed them—not that jealousies have hitherto caused any serious scandal, but lest in

[1] S. Bernardi Apologia ad Gulielmum.

striving for sobriety we lose the greater good of charity.

### Penitential Spirit.

There is one very wide difference between the abstinence from alcoholic liquor which has been encouraged in all ages in the Church, and that which in our own days has been so much commended by the sects. Abstinence in the Church was looked on as penal and satisfactory; but, owing to the prevalence of the Lutheran errors on justification, this view is little insisted on in modern temperance literature, even when it is not directly repudiated. By all means let us speak of temperance as a remedy, as a precaution, as a moral virtue, as an act of charity and self-denial, but let us not omit to treat it as an expiation. When the Catholic priest speaks to Catholics, there will be no difficulty in suggesting the practice of abstinence from a penitential spirit, *as a fast*, to appease the justice of God, and to propitiate His mercy. There are no doubt many cases in which total or partial abstinence, if imposed as a sacramental penance, at least for a time, would be willingly accepted and carefully fulfilled.

I would also respectfully suggest to those who have the guidance of souls and the confidence of our Catholic population, whether it would not be possible to take advantage of the great veneration still entertained for the fasts of the Church, to encourage a penitential abstinence from intoxicating drinks. I do not forget the concessions which prudence will require. There are weak stomachs, perhaps, which, without the aid of some moderate stimulant, could not bear a Lenten diet. In such cases St Augustin would say:—" If the weakness of the stomach cannot bear water, it is better to recruit it with a little wine, than to seek out unfermented drinks of a novel and expensive nature." [1]

There are also men whose labour is so exhausting that it would be a needless cruelty to deprive them of the "nourishment" which they *think* necessary for such labour; for the labouring poor have surely as much right to be humoured in their whims (if they are such) as dyspeptic gentlemen and nervous ladies. Yet, putting aside these cases, there are many men, unable from their hard labour to fast strictly, who willingly, when the suggestion is made to them, compensate by imposing on themselves some penitential restriction in the use of strong drinks. But, besides these, there are many at the present day who never eat meat on a day on which its use is forbidden by the Church, and who nevertheless drink to excess on Fridays

[1] Sermo 210, cap. 9.

and fast days no less than at other times. In the spirit of the Anglo-Saxon canon previously quoted,[1] it might be well to press on such men the inconsistency of their partial abstinence. The world ridicules them for their "superstitious" observance of abstinence from meat. The Church, on the contrary, would bid them complete that abstinence and make it useful and meritorious. The world would tell them to disobey the Church's law. The Church exhorts them to obey the law of God, prohibiting at all times excess in drink, as well as her own law, prohibiting at certain times the use of innocent food. Thus then, by putting frequently before the minds of the people that abstinence from strong drinks and moderation in their use are acts of Christian mortification, and therefore to be always associated in their minds with our Blessed Redeemer's Cross and His sacred Thirst; and by reminding those who have been guilty of excess that not merely reformation but contrition and satisfaction are required from them, and that the self-denial which they purpose to observe may and should be undertaken as a willing penance for past sin; and that penance is not a matter of which to boast but rather a matter of confusion; by imposing such self-denial in certain cases in connection with the graces of the

---

[1] See p. 65.

Sacrament of Penance; and by urging it on the attention of all in the Church's public penitential seasons, we shall cultivate a distinct Christian virtue, and draw down a blessing on the work from the Cross of our Divine Redeemer.

### AMUSEMENTS.

I would not be understood here to wish to connect the cause of temperance with gloom, and to dissociate it from popular amusements. On the contrary, were England more merry it would probably be less drunken. Men must have some relaxation, some excitement, some stimulant. There never was a people who required it more than those who dwell under our leaden canopies of cloud and smoke. There never was a time when it was half so necessary as now, when people toil in mines and factories and crowd in the filthy alleys of great cities. In Catholic England the town populations had their guilds with pageants and processions, and the country people their sports and pastimes. Recreation was not then associated in every man's mind, as it is now, with liquor, though intemperance got sometimes mixed up with it. But the connection of holidays and recreation with temperance is a very complex subject, and I prefer to omit altogether the notes I had gathered from past history, than to treat it inadequately and expose myself to misapprehension or retort. I would merely guard myself from being thought an enemy to amusements because I have advocated penance. "There is a time to weep, and a time to laugh; a time to mourn, and a time to dance; all things have their season" (Eccles. iii. 1-4).

## "The Help of Christians."

I would submit also to the consideration of pastors and confessors whether an old devotion might not be successfully revived in our own days under a new form, and for the special furtherance of sobriety.

A Scotch writer of the fourteenth century says:—" In the days of our fathers the Sabbath [*i.e.*, Saturday] was held in great veneration, in honour of the Blessed Virgin, principally by the devotion of women, who every Saturday, with great piety restricted themselves to one meal, and that merely of bread and water."[1]

Now any one acquainted with the manufacturing populations of our great cities must be aware that there is almost as much drunkenness on Saturday night as on all the other nights of the week together. The cause of this is, on the

[1] Fordun, Scotichronicon, lib. vii. cap. xlii.

one hand, the possession of the week's wages, and on the other the half holiday which has lately been introduced in these countries.

I am not of course so theoretical as to imagine that any considerable numbers of the toiling poor could be induced to undertake a fast on bread and water on the Saturday; nor could I bring myself to ask it of them even though they were willing. But I believe that very many would willingly, in honour of our Blessed Lady, either abstain altogether from the use of fermented and distilled drinks on that day, or at least would observe that abstinence from three o'clock on the Saturday afternoon, when the midday meal would be ended, until noon on Sunday. And I am sanguine enough to think that the propagation of this little act of piety would immensely diminish the amount of drunkenness among Catholics, and add immeasurably to the amount of domestic peace and comfort, and of spiritual health. As the Saturday fast was formerly called in England the Lady-Fast, so perhaps this act of abstinence might be called Our Lady's Abstinence. In proposing it to the people it would be important to explain that it is of the nature of a simple resolution, or that, if it is vowed, it is not under pain of mortal sin. The resolution or vow could be taken for life, or perhaps more prudently only for a year; from one feast of our Lady to another, or from one Communion to the next. There would be no need to make the resolution in presence of a priest. Each one could make or renew the offering before our Lady's altar in the church, or kneeling at home before her image; and as a memorial of it could wear her medal.

This act of piety is not of a nature to interfere with any association or good work already established, nor, if added as a supplement, would it in any way complicate their regulations.

I will only add one other remark on this suggestion. Fordun says, that the fast of Saturday originated "principally by the devotion of women." Perhaps Our Lady's Abstinence might be most effectually propagated by women; and so would repair an evil, which is certainly one of the most painful of modern scandals, I mean drunkenness amongst young women.

When Heli mistakenly reproached Anna for drunkenness, she replied: "Not so, my lord: for I am an exceeding unhappy woman, and have drank neither wine nor any strong drink. Count not thy handmaid for one of the *daughters of Belial*" (1 Kings i. 13–16). A woman given to drink was looked on in those days as a child of the devil. Alas in our own days girls of fourteen or fifteen years of age, earning independent wages in our factories, may be seen flocking together into beer-houses and gin shops, treating each other or accepting treats from men; and habitual drunkenness is not uncommon among girls in their teens.

But if Belial is multiplying his daughters, is not that a reason for the " Children of Mary " to redouble their activity? Let us get the good girls to propagate Our Lady's Abstinence among those of their own sex. It will soon spread amongst the men and sanctify the family.[1]

## THE YOUNG.

Perhaps, after all, the most effectual and fruitful method of attacking this devastating vice, will be to induce the young and innocent to band together against it. Clement of Alexandria wished that boys and girls should be as much as possible restricted from the use of fermented liquors. Many priests and bishops have most successfully induced the children to resolve not to touch such drinks until they are at least one-and-twenty years old. The children,

[1] I find that I have been anticipated in the above suggestion by the Rev. Kenelm Digby Beste, of the London Oratory. The Saturday Night Association was approved by the Archbishop of Westminster. See Appendix.

witnessing as they generally do the evils of drunkenness, and too often suffering from them in their own families, easily make this promise, and have no great difficulty in keeping it. While, if they are kept sober and virtuous to the age of one-and-twenty, good hopes may be entertained of their mature life.

### WORK BEFORE US.

These suggestions are not intended to be complete or exclusive. One lesson that we may learn from the past is, that the Church's methods are pliable, and that she is fertile in resources. Her discipline varied with circumstances. Though she is ever conservative and full of veneration for the ancient ways, yet it is their spirit rather than their form that she has retained. Her discipline has been like her architecture. It has not been identical in every country, though certain features were never wanting. One century did not servilely copy its predecessor, but developed what it had inherited into a character of its own. Of late indeed we have had no style belonging to ourselves, but copy, as fancy leads us, Egyptian and Greek, Byzantine and Gothic, while in doing so we are unfaithful to the lessons taught us equally by all the builders whom we venerate,

which were those of tradition and development,
opposed alike to servile reproduction and eccentric originality. This also is the lesson to be
drawn from our studies of the past in the region
of morals. I admire equally the Church of St
Theodore, that of St Anselm, and that of St
Edmund, but I admire them because, while
they faithfully retained the principles, sacraments, and discipline which are Catholic and
invariable, they studied the wants of their own
day, and met them by new developments.

Time, which leaves human nature unchanged,
has greatly changed the circumstances of our
spiritual warfare from those of our ancestors.
The population has been increased sixfold, and
is congregated in enormous cities, instead of
being scattered through villages and hamlets;
riches and poverty—both in their way incentives to intemperance, abound; the poor move
freely about instead of being confined to one
locality, and thus can evade both pastoral influence and that of public opinion and domestic
traditions; distilled spirits have replaced or
been added to the less intoxicating liquors of
former times; arts of poisonous adulteration
have been invented; facilities of manufacture,
and of transport, and of sale, have placed unnatural abundance and variety as a temptation in
every man's path; the fret of modern life, the

burden of excessive toil, the confinement of mines and factories, the absence of nearly all simple and healthful amusements for the poor, and the restraints of a puritanical Sabbath, all drive men to seek exhilaration in excessive use of stimulants. To meet these new conditions of life, and new temptations to intemperance, new methods have to be devised. To decide what methods are lawful, what prudent, belongs to the bishops of the Church, who are as watchful and as enlightened as their predecessors, and no less assisted by divine Wisdom. It is with profound submission to them that I conclude these notes by a quotation from the last address issued by the united episcopate of the venerable and most faithful Church of Ireland:—

"With deepest pain, and after the example of the Apostle weeping, we say, that the abominable vice of intemperance still continues to work dreadful havoc among our people, marring in their souls the work of religion, and in spite of their rare natural and supernatural virtues, changing many among them into enemies of the Cross of Christ, whose end is destruction; whose God is their belly, and whose glory is in their shame (Phil. iii. 18, 19). Is it not, dearly beloved, an intolerable scandal, that in the midst of a Catholic nation, like ours, there should be found so many slaves of intemperance, who habitually sacrifice to brutal excess in drinking not only their reason, but their character, the honour of their children, their substance, their health, their life, their souls, and God Himself? To drunkenness we may refer, as to its baneful cause, almost all the crime by which the country is disgraced, and much of the poverty from which it suffers. Drunkenness has wrecked more homes, once happy, than ever fell beneath the crowbar in the worst days of eviction: it has filled more graves and made more widows and orphans than did the famine; it has broken more hearts, blighted more hopes, and rent asunder family ties more ruthlessly, than the enforced exile to which their misery has condemned emigrants. Against an evil so widespread and so pernicious, we implore all who have at heart the honour of God and the salvation of souls, to be filled with holy zeal. We warn parents and employers that they are bound to set in their own persons an example of temperance to those who are subject to them, and to watch, lest through their own negligence, those entrusted to their charge should fall victims to drink. We exhort artisans and other members of the working classes, to join some one of the pious Confraternities approved of by the Church, in which, if they be faithful to the observance of their rules, they will find a school of

Christian self-denial. We bless from our hearts those zealous ecclesiastics, and others who, in accordance with the spirit of the Church, devote their time and energies to forwarding the cause of temperance; and we would remind all, that however valuable other helps may be, there exists but one unfailing source whence human weakness can draw strength to resist temptation, and break the bonds of evil habits. That source is the Sacred Heart of Jesus, the overflowing fountain of mercy, from which, through prayer and the sacraments, we receive grace in seasonable aid. The habit of daily prayer faithfully persevered in; frequent and worthy approach to the Holy Sacraments; the devout hearing of the Word of God; and the avoiding of dangerous occasions, are the only sure means by which intemperance can be overcome."[1]

[1] Pastoral Address of the Archbishops and Bishops of Ireland, at the close of the National Synod of Maynooth, 20th September 1875.

# APPENDIX.

I HAVE thought that it would be convenient to my clerical readers if I gave a summary of the principal Catholic organisations which have been lately set on foot in these countries. I cannot introduce them better than by

*The Words of the Cardinal Archbishop of Westminster.*

"Now, my dear friends, listen! I will go to my grave without tasting intoxicating liquors, but I repeat distinctly that any man who should say that the use of wine or any other like thing is sinful when it does not lead to drunkenness, that man is a heretic condemned by the Catholic Church. With that man I will never work. Now, I desire to promote total abstinence in every way that I can; I will encourage all societies of total abstainers. But the moment I see men not charitable attempting to trample down those who do not belong to the total abstainers, from that moment I will not work with those men.

"I would have two kinds of pledge—one for the

mortified who never taste drink, and the other for the temperate who never abuse it. If I can make these two classes work together, I will work in the midst of them. If I cannot get them to work together, I will work with both of them separately.[1]

*Words of the Archbishops and Bishops of Ireland.*

The Bishops of Ireland, in their public meeting of October 1873, unanimously passed the following resolution :—"That we earnestly call upon our clergy throughout Ireland to exert all their vigilance and zeal in repressing drunkenness, which is one of the greatest evils of the day, demoralising and impoverishing the people, and destroying in thousands the souls which Christ died to save. Amongst the means which may be usefully employed, we recommend 'The Association of Prayer,' and the establishment in every parish of Temperance Societies, based upon the principles of the Catholic religion."

[1] From an address to the members of the Holy Family Confraternity, at St Mary's and St Michael's, Commercial Road, in 1875.

## I.

### CONFRATERNITY OF THE SACRED THIRST AND AGONY OF JESUS, AND OF THE DOLOURS OF MARY, TO REPRESS INTEMPERANCE.

*Erected by His Holiness Pope Pius IX. into a Confraternity, August 30, 1874, and approved of by all the Bishops of England, Ireland, and Scotland.*

"Afterwards, Jesus said, I thirst; and they gave him vinegar to drink mingled with gall."—S. JOHN and S. MATTHEW.

#### OBJECT.

This Confraternity has for its object the union of all the faithful, *especially of those who are in the friendship of God*, in devotion to the Sacred Thirst and Agony of Jesus, and the Compassionate Heart of Mary, to obtain the repression of the brutalising vice of intemperance, which, as St John Chrysostom tells us, is the "joy of demons, and the parent of ten thousand evils."

#### MEANS.

I. Each member shall recite daily, "Our Father" once, and "Hail Mary" three times in honour of the Sacred Thirst and Agony of Jesus, and of the Compassionate Heart of Mary, for the intentions of the Confraternity, and the repression of this awful vice.

II. All are requested to offer their other good works for this purpose, especially Holy Communion on the 2nd Sunday of the month. This offering, far from taking away or diminishing the efficacy of these good works for other intentions, will greatly increase it.

III. As "Prayer is good with fasting and alms," (*Tobias* xii. 8.), the zealous are recommended to add some small act of mortification, especially in the use of drinks on Fridays, or oftener, if their devotion suggests it.

IV. Some alms can be given for the same purpose.

No money, however, is demanded; but if any person wishes to help on this good work, and to have a larger share in its blessings, he can contribute to defray the necessary expenses of printing, &c., which have exceeded, up to November 1874, £1400.

No pledge is required. No duty is obligatory under sin.

### Conditions.

To be a Catholic, and to be duly enrolled.

### Advantages.

His Holiness has granted (August 30th, 1874) to this work of charity the following indulgences:—

*Partial.*—3 years and 3 quarantines each time the prayers prescribed are said; and 7 years and 7 quarantines if they are said in common.

300 days for each act of mortification done for the intentions of the Confraternity.

300 days for enrolling a member; and 7 years and 7 quarantines for enrolling ten.

100 days for the ejaculation, "O Lord Jesus, through Thy most Sacred Thirst, save us."

*Plenary.*—On condition that the members, being truly penitent, after going to Confession and receiving worthily Holy Communion, visit a Church of the Confraternity, and pray for some time for the propagation of the Faith, and for the intention of the Sovereign Pontiff; on the day of enrolment, and on the Feasts of the Most Precious Blood, of the Holy Name, and of the Five Wounds of our Lord; of the Most Pure Heart, of the Seven Dolours and the Auxilium Christianorum of the B. Virgin Mary; of the Patronage of St Joseph, of St George, Patron of England; of St Patrick, Patron of Ireland; and of St Andrew, Patron of Scotland.

### ORGANISATION.

I. The Confraternity is governed, under the Director, by the parish priests and heads of Religious Houses, or their delegates, as Local Directors.

II. Zelators aid in spreading the devotion by enrolling members and inscribing their names on Zelator Cards. For this purpose they receive from the Local Director Zelator sets, each of which contains ten prints, six leaflets, and one Zelator Card. To every member a print is given, as billet of membership, and to all who can read, a leaflet.

III. All names on the Zelator Cards should be written out in a special registry kept for the purpose. Each branch affiliated is entitled to keep such a registry.

IV. All children should be enrolled.

"I recommend you especially to *propagate this devotion in our Schools*, that the minds of our youth may, from their opening years, be impressed with the liveliest sentiments of the enormity of the vice of intemperance, and that their example and prayers may continually remind their parents, and those around them, of the all-importance and blessings of temperance."—*Letter of His Eminence to the Very Rev. Dr Spratt, February* 24*th* 1869.

V. In order to keep the duties of the Confraternity before the minds of the members, on the second Sunday of each month, at a meeting to be held, or at Mass, the prayers prescribed above should be recited, a report read, and a short exhortation delivered.

That reports may be drawn up, the Local Directors are requested to communicate any well-authenticated edifying fact, or any conversion, or striking example, they may hear of or know, as also the number of the associates enrolled.

Letters, &c., should be addressed—THE DIRECTOR, CONFRATERNITY OF PRAYER, UPPER GARDINER STREET, DUBLIN.

ILLUSTRATED NEWSPAPER.

Each family should take the "Illustrated Monitor," which, for the present, appears twice a month. Being the organ of the Confraternity, it is hoped that it will remind the members of their duties. It costs three halfpence a copy, or, by post, 4s. per annum—in America, 1 dol. 25 cents—and may be obtained from Mr Dollard, 13 and 14 Dame Street, Dublin, by whom special terms are made when a large number is ordered.

## II.
## THE LEAGUE OF THE CROSS
*(A Total Abstinence Association).*

### OBJECTS.

To promote the greater glory of God and elevate the religious and social state of our people by the suppression of intemperance ; the formation of a sound public opinion on this question ; and the cordial union of all Catholics, both clergy and laity, in a warfare against drunkenness, and the drinking habits of society.

### MEANS.

The means to be employed are Prayer and the Sacraments of the Church, Confraternities, the total abstinence pledge, meetings, lectures, the public press, pamphlets, entertainments, good example of the members, inducing others to join in the movement, and the formation of branches of the League wherever practicable.

For the spiritual benefit and temporal welfare of the members, the Holy Sacrifice of the Mass will be offered by the president of each branch once a month, for which an offering will be made by the branch.

Members are recommended to approach Holy Communion once every month, and in a body, if the rector of the mission shall deem it advisable.

### THE PLEDGE.

The following is the pledge of the Total Abstinence

League of the Cross; on taking which the people kneel down in front of the priest, and in an audible voice recite after him :—

"I promise to you, Father, and to the League of the Holy Cross, by the help of God's grace, to abstain from all intoxicating drinks, and to discourage the use of them as much as possible."

After taking the pledge each person is presented with the book of rules, and, after a month from joining, with the card of membership. The card is signed by the priest, who is president of the district, *and must be returned if the pledge is broken.* He is entitled to wear the Cross of the League so long as he remains a practical teetotaller, but no longer.

1. The pledge of total abstinence binds all who take it to abstain from all intoxicating drinks, cider, cordials, and liqueurs.

2. If a medical adviser should direct a member to take intoxicating drink in time of sickness, he ought to make known to him that he has taken the pledge.

3. If any medical man shall nevertheless insist upon his taking any intoxicating drink as medicine, he may do so, in obedience to his authority, during the continuance of the sickness.

4. On recovery any one who shall continue to take intoxicating drink, under whatsoever plea, would thereby break the pledge, which he must renew if he wishes to continue a member of the League of the Cross.

It is strongly recommended that the members of the League shall do all they can to encourage those who are not prepared to take the total abstinence pledge to bind themselves not to drink in public-houses, or enter them without strict necessity.

## THE BRANCHES.

In each mission in which a branch of the League shall be established, the rector of the mission, or other clergyman appointed by him, shall be president of such branch; and no branch shall be established until the rector of the mission in which it is proposed to be established shall have consented to become president, or agreed to appoint one thereto.

## VISITORS AND THEIR DUTIES.

As one of the most important means of securing success is the house-to-house visitation, so, also, one of the most important duties in connection with the League devolves upon the visitors deputed by each branch, and therefore the greatest discrimination and care should be exercised in appointing the members thereof. The duty to be performed is not only of a very delicate nature, but requires considerable zeal, tact, good sense, and affability, and should on no account be neglected, or hurriedly performed.

When a branch has been established in a mission, the first thing to be done is to divide the mission into sub-districts, each sub-district comprising two, three, or six streets, according as the branch committee may deem advisable; always having in view that the greater the number of sub-districts, and the fewer the streets in each, the more efficiently and easily will the work be performed, and the more reliable the statistics founded on the visitor's report.

To each of these sub-districts, two visitors, supplied with a pocket register, or book containing the names and addresses of the members resident therein, shall be appointed by the branch committee; and their duty will be to visit the people in their homes, exhort good members to continue steadily in the path they have chosen, encourage wavering ones to perseverance; and induce, if possible, others residing in the same house to become members of the League, pointing to the improved condition of their neighbours who have already joined the movement, as convincing evidence of the good it has done, and is capable of doing, when its rules are faithfully carried out. By these means the people will see that in joining the ranks of the League they have not only an opportunity of shaking off bad habits and acquiring new and good ones, but that they may promote their happiness and that of their families, and become respectable and useful members of society, and thoroughly practical Catholics.

For further information regarding the organisation of the League of the Cross, I must refer the reader to the book of rules published by R. Washbourne, 18 Paternoster Row, London. The League and its rules have the approbation of His Eminence, the Cardinal Archbishop of Westminster.

## III.
## THE SALFORD DIOCESAN CRUSADE;
*Consisting of the Total Abstinence League, and the Association of Prayer.*

#### CONSTITUTION AND RULES.

##### PATRONS.

The Crusade is consecrated to our Blessed REDEEMER, in memory of His painful THIRST and AGONY on the Cross.

It is under the patronage of our Blessed Mother, QUEEN of SORROWS;

Of ST JOSEPH, head and guardian of the HOLY FAMILY, and patron of home life;

Of ST JOHN the Baptist, and ST JAMES the Apostle, called "the Brother of our Lord" and "the Just," both of whom from a spirit of penance and mortification were total abstainers all the days of their lives.

It is under the jurisdiction of the Lord Bishop of the Diocese.

##### OBJECTS.

The objects of the Crusade are—

1. To promote and repair the honour of our Divine Creator, shamefully outraged through sins of intemperance by the creatures whom He has redeemed; and

2. To improve the spiritual and social condition of the people, by a cordial union of all Catholics, clergy and laity, in a holy crusade against the drinking and intemperate habits of society.

### MEANS.

The habit of self-indulgence can only be cured by a habit of self-denial, which is a law of the gospel, and a fruit of Divine grace. The divinely-appointed means of grace are Prayer and the Sacraments, which assist us to make good resolutions, and enable us to keep them. The Crusade, therefore, in the first place, unites in an " Association of Prayer in honour of the Sacred THIRST and AGONY of our Blessed Redeemer," to which it will cultivate a special devotion. Prayer and the Sacraments are its supernatural weapons. To these it adds mutual brotherly support, by the formation of a "Total Abstinence League;" the creation of a strong public opinion against the vice of drunkenness, by means of public meetings, lectures, entertainments, and the use of the press; and the regular and solemn administration of the total abstinence pledge, which may be justly called a spiritual and heroic act of mortification.

### MEMBERSHIP.

This Society shall consist of all persons who are willing to promote the honour of God by uniting in a holy crusade against the drinking and intemperate habits of society.

The ORDINARY MEMBERS are those who from whatsoever cause do not bind themselves by the pledge, yet are willing to co-operate with those who are pledged, by the practice of prayer and of mortification in honour of the Sacred THIRST and AGONY of our Lord. They will be enrolled in the Crusade's Association of Prayer in honour of the Sacred THIRST, and will receive the white card of admission, and be entitled to wear the badge of the Crusade. They will also attend the religious services of the society whenever they can, and forward the movement by all means in their power. They have a right to attend all open meetings, and with the permission of the president to speak at them; but they shall have no vote, unless they have been elected to fill offices or to sit on committees. They are invited to pay one halfpenny a week towards the expenses of the Crusade.

The PLEDGED MEMBERS are those who have taken the total abstinence pledge, and pay one penny a week towards the working expenses. They should also be enrolled in the Association of Prayer in honour of the Sacred THIRST, and attend the religious services. They are entitled to wear the badge of the Crusade, and the total abstainer's medal; to speak at all open meetings, with the consent of the president, and to record their vote.

Let, therefore, members of this society reflect upon the multitudes who from drink, or neglect, or ignorance, are wanderers, astray and out of their Church. Let them take the words of the Lord as addressed to themselves:—"*Behold I will send many fishers, saith the Lord, and they shall fish them; and after this I will send many hunters, and they shall hunt them from every mountain and from every hill, and out of the holes of the rocks*" (Jer. xvi.) And again, "*Jesus said, Come after Me, and I will make you to become fishers of men*" (Mark i. 17).

## THE FISHERS AND HUNTERS.

Though all, the ORDINARY as well as the PLEDGED members, should exercise their zeal and brotherly charity by endeavouring to bring souls to the Church, yet a certain number shall be told off in each branch to be called the "FISHERS AND HUNTERS" of the Crusade.

Each branch will divide the streets in its mission among their FISHERS and HUNTERS, who shall be persons nominated for their prudence, tact, and good sense, so that no just offence be given to the persons whom they may visit.

The duties of the FISHERS and HUNTERS will be,

1. To enrol in the "Association of Prayer in honour of the Sacred THIRST and AGONY of Our LORD" all who are willing to take upon themselves its obligations. For this they shall be furnished by the committee of their branch with a register and the white cards of admission.

2. To visit the pledged members in their houses, and to encourage them to persevere, and to induce others to take the pledge.

3. To circulate from house to house the little monthly periodical, called "The Monitor of the Association of Prayer," and the papers of the "Catholic Truth Society," and others that may be determined on, and to collect and exchange them at the end of the week.

4. To encourage the reading of good books by endeavouring to circulate the books of a Catholic Lending or Popular Library, where one exists.

5. To induce parents to send their children to school, and to persuade such Catholics as may be living in the neglect of their duty, to frequent the Church and the Sacraments.

6. Finally, to hold themselves ready to co-operate with the clergy in the promotion of all good works for the salvation of souls.

Each FISHER and HUNTER should keep a note of the work he has done, and should give an account of it to the Chaplain-president from time to time, especially when it concerns the bringing of children to school and of people to their religious duties.

### MOTIVES FOR TAKING THE PLEDGE.

There are various motives for taking the total abstinence pledge, which must commend it to the respect and approval of all Catholics.

1. Its absolute necessity for those who without it cannot overcome the tyranny of the passion for drink.

2. The wonderful power of good example to encourage and sustain those who are tempted to break their pledge and plunge into all manner of excess; and the unspeakable value of self-denial in the eyes of God, when undertaken through pure charity and love for the brotherhood.

3. As an heroic act of mortification, following in respect of drink the example of those religious orders who, from a spirit of Christian mortification, with the formal approval and blessing of the Church, pledge themselves to abstain from the use of flesh-meat.

4. As a protest against the general abuse of in-

toxicating liquors, and as an act of reparation to the injured Majesty of God for the sins of drunkenness committed in this country, especially by our fellow-Catholics.

5. In memory of all that our dear Lord endured for our sins, and especially of His Sacred THIRST and AGONY on the Cross, when He suffered His mouth and palate to be drenched for our sake with vinegar and gall.

### THE PLEDGE.

The following is the form of Pledge to be used by the Crusade. It must be recited kneeling, in an audible voice, before the Priest:

> "*I promise, by the grace of God, and with the prayers of the Immaculate and Blessed Virgin and S. Joseph, to abstain from all intoxicating drinks, and to discountenance their use as far as possible.*"

Each person taking the Pledge will receive a card of association, on which will be written his or her name and address in full, and the date of admittance into the League. The card is to be signed by the president of the branch. After three months' probation the name will be registered by the secretary in the Great Book of the Crusade.

Priests administering the pledge in the Church or in private houses are respectfully invited to take the name and address of the persons to whom they give it, and hand them to one of the officers of the

Crusade, who will visit and invite them to join their ranks.

As there unhappily exists in this country a heresy in respect to the nature and use of spirituous liquors, and as the "Salford Diocesan Crusade" is determined, above all things, to preserve inviolate the True Faith, without which it is impossible to please God, it hereby enters its protest against even the suspicion of heretical teaching. Every member of the Crusade, therefore, declares that he heartily rejects and anathematises the detestable heresy of the Manichees—condemned by the Church fifteen centuries ago—which teaches that spirituous liquors are not creatures of God, that they are intrinsically evil, and that whoever uses them is thereby guilty of sin. No person can be a member of the "Salford Crusade against the vice of Intemperance" who does not from his heart reject this and every other heresy condemned by our Holy Mother the Church.

### RELIGIOUS FUNCTIONS OF THE CRUSADE.

It would be well that every mission branch should attend a Religious Service and Benediction in their own Church, once a-week, if possible, and this more especially if any prayers are said or instruction given specially for the benefit of the Crusade.

It is also desired that all the members should approach Holy Communion on the second Sunday of every month.

The Religious Festivals of the Crusade shall be the Feasts of the FIVE PRECIOUS WOUNDS in Lent, of the SEVEN DOLOURS in September; of ST JOSEPH in

March; of the BEHEADING OF ST JOHN THE BAPTIST in August, and of ST JAMES in May, or the Sundays following these Feasts.

Where it is possible, there should be held, once a quarter in some large church, a District Meeting of all the members, ORDINARY and PLEDGED, belonging to the district, under the direction of the district-president. When the district-president so directs, the members will go to these religious functions wearing the badge of the Crusade; and if there be a procession, each branch should carry its own banner, and the whole procession should be headed by the banner of the district.

For further particulars regarding this Association, I must refer to the Rules, approved by the Bishop of Salford.

## IV.

### THE CRUSADE; OR, CATHOLIC ASSOCIATION FOR THE SUPPRESSION OF DRUNKENNESS.

*Under the Protection of our Blessed Lady of the Immaculate Conception.*

I am sorry that I have not space to reprint the whole of the Rev. Father Richardson's book.[1] I must be satisfied with a few extracts, giving the scope and principal rules of the Crusade.

[1] Published by R. Washbourne, 18A Paternoster Row, London.

### Object.

It may perhaps be as well to state in the beginning that this is not exclusively a society of reformed drunkards, but a pious association of Catholics, who, relying upon the help of God's grace, and the powerful intercession of the Immaculate Mother of God, have *resolved to use every legitimate effort for the suppression of drunkenness.*

Let no one therefore excuse himself from joining, under the plea that he is not a drunkard. The enemy is a *common* one—it is the enemy of our religion; the enemy of our salvation—the enemy of our God; and THAT ENEMY IS DRUNKENNESS—NOT DRINK, BUT DRUNKENNESS.

### Rules.

I. Any Catholic of any age may be enrolled.

II. To begin the work in the grace of God by going to confession (if necessary) about the time of entering.

III. To say devoutly, nine times every day, for the perseverance of the members and the conversion of drunkards, "*O Mary, conceived without sin, pray for us who have recourse to thee.*"

IV. To embrace and faithfully observe one of the following rules about drinking.

### Total Abstinence.

To abstain from ALL KINDS *of intoxicating liquors* for the love of God, your own spiritual and temporal welfare, and that of your neighbour.

To try to induce your children, and those under your charge, to do the same.

The members are to hold themselves bound to this promise, even after failing, until they have asked for and obtained a dispensation from their confessor.

Total abstainers must have "Total" marked upon their card, and wear scarlet cord or ribbon for their medal.

### Partial Abstinence.

Never to drink in a public-house, except when taking a meal.

As it is impossible to legislate for every case by rule, the president can allow whatever he thinks good for a member, or forbid whatever he thinks hurtful, provided the end of the society be attained, and this stated on the member's card.

### Officers.

The president should be a priest, and have the entire management of the association. He can dismiss and appoint officers, and make such alterations in the rules as the nature of the locality may require.

He may even change the name of the association, call it a Guild, Confraternity, or Club,[1] or place it under the protection of any other Saint. The members

---

[1] It is recommended not to call it a "temperance society," as it is quite distinct from societies of that name generally, being more of a Catholic fraternity with a specific object in view.

will still belong to the "*Crusade*," if only the following be left intact :—

That they wear a medal of the Immaculate Conception.

Promise not to go beyond a fixed quantity of intoxicating liquor.

Renew this promise at least four times in the year before a priest.

That there be some one to watch over the fidelity of the members.

That the date and card of admission be changed upon the failure of a member, on his promising to go to the Sacraments.

The president shall preside over all meetings,[1] or appoint some one else.

---

## V.

## HOLY LEGION OF PRAYER,

*For the suppression of drunkenness, and especially to ask God's blessing on all societies engaged in this holy work.*

### Rules.

I. To recite daily seven times the "Ave Maria" in memory of the sorrows of the Immaculate Heart of

---

[1] These meetings are not absolutely necessary but extremely useful, especially at starting, and should be held about once in six weeks, *not at fixed times*, but called when there is anything of interest to communicate to the members, and, if possible, should be a little before Feast Days.

Mary during the thirst of her Divine Son upon the Cross.

II. To select and offer for the ends of this Legion one or more of the following practices of mortification or piety :—

1. Offer or procure to be offered annually the Holy Sacrifice.
2. A monthly Communion.
3. Unite with great *patience* all you may suffer from hunger, cold, thirst, or sickness with the sorrowful heart of Mary.
4. Abstain absolutely from drinking between meals.
5. Abstain on Saturdays from all intoxicating liquors.
6. Abstain for a whole year and renew again this resolution by going to the Sacrament the week before it expires, or embrace some other act.
7. Abstain from all kinds of spirits as above for a whole year.
8. Never to enter a public-house on Saturday night or the whole of Sunday.
9. Assist weekly at a week-day Mass, and pray for those in danger of falling.

Any other special act of mortification may be adopted, *e.g.*, not to take more than one pint in a day, or two pints, or to abstain totally for life, or for seven years, &c.

## VI.

### SATURDAY NIGHT ASSOCIATION IN HONOUR OF OUR BLESSED LADY.[1]

The object of the association is the performance of an act of abstinence upon Saturday in honour of the Mother of God, and in reparation of the many sins of intemperance by which the day dedicated to her is dishonoured.

The associates engage to abstain from beer and spirits after their dinner on Saturday until their dinner on Sunday.

---

## VII.

### THE HOLY WAR AGAINST DRUNKENNESS.

"This kind goeth not out but by prayer and fasting."—
MATT. xvii. 20.

This Holy War is a united attack upon drinking habits, which are far more difficult to overcome than drunkenness itself; they are bound up with the manners and customs of our people, and it will require great energy and determination on the part of the members to con-

---

[1] This association, established in Brompton by the Rev. K. D. Beste, has the approval of the Archbishop of Westminster. Father Beste published a very interesting Address to the association, which can be obtained from Dillon, 2 Alexander Place, Brompton, London.

tend successfully against them. Our weapons are prayer, fasting, and alms.

1. *Prayer.*—The constant oblations of the Holy Mass and the *De profundis* daily offered up by all the members, especially for the repose of the souls of those who are now suffering in purgatory, either on account of having sinned mortally by intemperance, and afterwards repented, or of having in any way clouded the intelligence by drink, or taken more than was good for health, or encouraged others to do so. These souls now know the sad consequences of such sins, and will be our best helpers in this conflict.

2. *Fasting.*—The mortification which the members embrace will be, not to drink in a public-house[1] or refreshment-bar of any kind, and they will offer this act of mortification and inconvenience for the relief of the suffering souls as above.

3. *Alms.*—To make a small offering weekly for masses for the perseverance of the members, and the repose of the souls in purgatory, according to the intention of the rule.

RULES.

1. Never to drink in a public-house.
2. To say *De profundis* or three Paters every night.
3. To offer one halfpenny *weekly*.
4. To wear openly a small cross.

This war is not intended to interfere in any way with the League of the Cross, but to receive only those who are unwilling to embrace total abstinence.

---

[1] Except when staying in or taking a meal at an hotel.

FORM OF ADMISSION.

After obtaining a card of rules, to accept a Cross of the Holy War from any priest, with the intention of keeping the rule, *until the card has been returned to the priest from whom it was received.*[1]

## VIII.

## GERMAN TEMPERANCE ASSOCIATION.

There exists in some parts of Germany a Temperance Association, the statutes of which were approved by His Holiness Pius IX. on 28th July 1851, and enriched with indulgences.

1. The members bind themselves for life to total abstinence from all distilled spirits.

2. They promise sobriety in the use of fermented drinks.

3. They undertake to propagate the Association.

The form of promise, pronounced before an altar in the presence of the director, is as follows:—

"I promise before Almighty God, the Blessed Virgin Mary, my angel guardian, and all the saints, to abstain from all distilled liquors, and to be sober in the use of fermented ones. I will also endeavour

---

[1] *Coadjutors* having a red card undertake to urge as many as possible to join the Holy War, and to discourage all kinds of drinking for conviviality.

to bring my neighbours to this Confraternity, to the best of my power.

"At the same time, I acknowledge that I should be guilty of unfaithfulness to God, and deserve disgrace with men, and exclusion from this Confraternity, if I should presume for frivolous reasons to violate this holy promise which I have made knowingly and freely."

4. The associates engage to recite, at least on Sundays and holydays, the Memorare or three Hail Marys.

5. The Titular Feast is the Purification, on which day there should be a High Mass and sermon; and a requiem for deceased members as soon afterwards as possible.

6. Plenary indulgences may be gained on the day of admission, at death, on the Feast of the Purification, and four other feasts to be appointed once for all by the bishop of each diocese. There are also many partial indulgences.

# INDEX.

ABSTINENCE, praised by Clement, 2; Origen, 4, 5; St Augustin, 8, 61; St Bernard, 9, 60; Julianus Pomerius, 18; St Gildas, 19; St Isidore of Pelusium, 20; St Antiochus, 20; Nicetas, 20; St Chrysostom, 58; St Jerome, 58; St Edmund, 67; St Boniface, 77; Bl. Humbert, 60-62; practised by saints, 9, 58, 102, 103, 241; of clergy, 58; of ascetics, 60-62; of penitents, 72; of the young, 225; of Lent, 65, 219; penal, 72, 135, 142, 145; freely accepted, 154-157; requires grace, 202 (*see* Discipline, Pledge, Association, Penance); false, 4, 8, 18-22, 202, 209; Our Lady's, 223

Adulteration, 123

Ælfric, his homilies, 130; his canons, 150

Ælred, St, quoted, 211

Ale. *See* Beer.

Ales, 106-117; scot-ales (*see* Scotales); bid-ales, 107; bride-ales, 108; church-ales, 111-114; dove-ales, 108; Easter and Whitsun ales, 111; give-ales, 109; help-ales, 108; king's-ales, 116

Alphonsus, St, quoted, 76

Amusements, 221

Anselm, St, his abstinence, 58; his laws, 168

R

Aqua vitæ. *See* Spirits
Asceticism defended, 11-17
Associations, importance of, 214; variety of, 215-217, 231; rules of, 233-256; dangerous, 201-203
Augustin, St, on true abstinence, 8, 219; on drunkenness, 24-44; on temptations, 210

BEDE, VENERABLE, 132; his letter, 146; his canons, 148
Beer in England, 79, 84, 188; in Scotland, 121; assize of, 120, 125-128
Beer-houses, 120-123, 185, 190, 194. *See* Taverns
Bernard, St, on true and false abstinence, 9, 10, 63; on generosity, 60, 62; on good novelties, 206; on charity in diversity, 216
Boasting, 19, 217
Boniface, St, his letter, 77; his abstinence, 58
Britannia, curious derivation of, 85
British Church, 76, 134-136
Britons given to drunkenness, 76, 85

CÆSARIUS, ST, of Arles, his sermons, 44-48; his treatment of confirmed drunkards, 68; his exhortation to penitents, 157, 209
Campion, the martyr, quoted, 81, 94, 95
Canons of African Council, 30; of British Church, 134; of Irish Church, 141, 180-183; of Anglo-Saxon Church, 145; of Council of Lateran, 169; of English Councils, 170-178; of Scotch Church, 172
Capital crime, drunkenness when a, 71, 148
Challenging to drink, 46, 104, 135, 142, 169
Charity in diversity, 216-218
Charity dinners, 113, 117
Charta Forestæ, 170
Churches, drinking in, 31-44, 105, 149
Civil power, 199; its action in England, 118-129, 184-191
Clergy, discipline of, 53-59; drunkenness among, 24, 49, 57, 70, 77, 80, 146, 150, 169; not all priests, 174

*Index.* 259

Confraternity. *See* Associations
Councils against drunkenness recommended by St Augustin, 28, and by St Boniface, 77; of Clovesho, 147, 163; of Lateran, 169; of St Alban's, 170; frequent in England, 168; in Scotland, 172; in Ireland, 180–182
Crusade against drunkenness, 215, 241, 248
Cummian, St, 138; his Penitential, 139, 141
Custom, force of, 38, 45, 49
Customs of drinking, 99

DANES in England, 77, 105
David, St, 134, 137
Discipline varies, 226–228; of clergy, 53; of ascetics, 59; of laity, 62
Drunkenness described, 46, 50, 148; common in early ages of Church, 23; not peculiar to northern climates, 75; in Africa, 24; in Gaul, 44; in Germany, 49; in England, 75–78, 188–195; in Ireland, 79–81, 228; in Scotland, 96; rare in Italy, 75, 77; amongst clergy, 24, 150 (*see* Clergy); in churches, 27, 151; causes of, 73, 200, 227; when a capital crime, 71, 148; how punished by Church, *see* Canons, Councils, Penance; not punished by civil power before Reformation, 167; afterwards by fines, 191; whipping, 192; remedies for, *see* Abstinence, Association, Pledge
Dunstan, St, 105; his code, 149; his Treatise on Penance, 160, 164

EDGAR, KING, his law, 78, 105; his code, 149
Edmund, St, his advice, 67; his canons, 173
Egbert, Archbishop, 148, 156
English given to excess, 75

FABYAN, the chronicler, 109, 179
Fasting defended, 13–17; true observance of, 8; abstinence from drink, 65–67, 219
Feasting, 17, 47, 50, 89, 99–103
Funerals, doles at, 29, 110, 178, 181. *See* Wakes

GILDAS, ST, explains true abstinence, 19; accuses Britons of intemperance, 76; his canons, 135; visits Ireland, 137
Giraldus Cambrensis, his testimony about Irish intemperance examined, 79–81
Good Templars, 11, 202
Grace before drinking, 101, 103
Grace needed for abstinence, 202–204
Gregory, St, his advice to St Mellitus, 64; on penance, 69
Grosseteste, Robert, 172

HEALTHS, drinking of, 104
Heresies on subject of abstinence, 7, 8, 9, 21, 202, 231
Humbert, Blessed, 60, 61
Hydromel, 87, 109

INNOCENT III., POPE, his joke about the English, 79
Intemperance. *See* Drunkenness
Ireland, what Giraldus says about, 79, 81; refuted, 80, 81; drinks used in, 92–95
Irish Church, 79–82, 136–144
Isidore of Pelusium, St, 20
Italy, drunkenness rare in, 75, 76

JAMES, ST, the Just, 58, 241
Jerome, St, 58
JESUS CHRIST, His teaching and example explained, 3, 7, 11–15; His sacred thirst, 231, 241
John Baptist, St, 11–14, 241
John of Salisbury, 78, 89, 101

LAITY, discipline of, 62
Lent, fast of, 8, 64, 219
Licences, 120, 185, 190–192

MARGARET, ST, anecdote of, 103
Mead, 84, 87
Metheglin, 87, 189

Mohammedans, their abstinence, 55, 60, 80
Moran, Bishop, quoted, 137, 180-183

NAZARENES or Nazarites, 55, 60
Normans in England, 78, 100

OBITS, 109-111. *See* Funerals
Our Lady. *See* Virgin Mary
Origen on abstinence, 4

PATRON FEASTS, 181
Pegs, drinking to, 78, 105, 169
Penance, 152-166, 218-221; sacrament of, 69-74. *See* Canons
Pledge, the, in what sense ancient, 53, 206; those of St Edmund, 67, and St Cæsarius, 68; forms of 246, 255; purpose of, 208, 209, 245; obligation of, 214; violation of, 144; abuse of, 208, 211
Pledging. *See* Challenging
Plunkett, Archbishop, 82, 182
Prayer, importance of, 211, 233, 242, 251
Preaching against drunkenness, 26, 44, 131
Priests. *See* Clergy
Pullen, Cardinal, 15

RABANUS MAURUS, his sermons, 49
Rechabites, 60
Religious Orders, discipline of, 59

SACRAMENT OF PENANCE. *See* Penance
Saturday, fast on, 222; abstinence on, 223, 253
Scotales, meaning of, 107; in forest lands, 171; canons against, 172-176. *See* Ales
Scotland, drinks used in, 95-97; ancient laws of, 119-123; council in, 172
Sermons. *See* Preaching
Spirits, little used until sixteenth century, 92; their use in Ireland, 81, 92-94, 182; in Scotland, 96, 97; in England, 188; abstinence from, in Germany, 255

Sumptuary laws, 101, 186
Sunday-closing, 178, 179
Synods. *See* Canons, Councils

TASTERS, 121–123
Taverns, 122, 150, 174, 176, 180, 185, 194. *See* Beer-houses
Temperance. *See* Abstinence
Temperance Associations. *See* Associations
Theodore, St, 145, 159
Thirst, Confraternity of Sacred, 233, 241
Thomas, St, of Canterbury, anecdote of, 86
Thomas, St, of Aquin, quoted, 144
Timothy, St, his abstinence, 58

USQUEBAUGH. *See* Spirits

VIRGIN MARY, abstinence in honour of, 222, 256; by help of, 233, 241, 248

WAKES of saints, 105, 151; of dead, 106, 110, 150, 173, 177
Water drunk as penance, 84, 143, 145; supposed to be unhealthy, 83
Whisky. *See* Spirits
Willibrod, St, 145
Wine, 87–92, 124–129, 186–188
Wulstan, St, anecdote of, 102

# THE DISCIPLINE OF DRINK.

PRINTED BY BALLANTYNE, HANSON AND CO.
EDINBURGH AND LONDON

THE

# DISCIPLINE OF DRINK:

An Historical Inquiry into the Principles and Practice
of the Catholic Church

REGARDING THE

## USE, ABUSE, AND DISUSE OF ALCOHOLIC LIQUORS,

*Especially in England, Ireland, and Scotland,
from the 6th to the 16th Century.*

BY THE

REV. T. E. BRIDGETT,

OF THE CONGREGATION OF THE MOST HOLY REDEEMER.

*PERMISSU SUPERIORUM.*

With an Introductory Letter to the Author,

BY

HIS EMINENCE CARDINAL MANNING,

ARCHBISHOP OF WESTMINSTER.

LONDON:
BURNS AND OATES,
17 AND 18 PORTMAN STREET, AND 63 PATERNOSTER ROW.
1876.

www.ingramcontent.com/pod-product-compliance
Lightning Source LLC
Chambersburg PA
CBHW032112230426
43672CB00009B/1705